Bibliotheca topographica Britannica. No IX. Containing sketches of the history and antiquities of the parish of Stoke Newington, in the county of Middlesex.

Bibliotheca topographica Britannica. No IX. Containing sketches of the history and antiquities of the parish of Stoke Newington, in the county of Middlesex.
Multiple Contributors, See Notes
ESTCID: T079958
Reproduction from British Library
Anonymous. By James Brown. In: "Bibliotheca topographica Britannica" (vol.2, part 2). Half-title: 'No IX. Sketches of the history and antiquities of the parish of Stoke Newington, .. '. Numbered No.10 in Nichols' list of 1790. With a final errata leaf
London : printed by and for J. Nichols, 1783.
[4],53,[1]p.,plate,table : ill. ; 4°

Eighteenth Century
Collections Online
Print Editions

Gale ECCO Print Editions

Relive history with *Eighteenth Century Collections Online*, now available in print for the independent historian and collector. This series includes the most significant English-language and foreign-language works printed in Great Britain during the eighteenth century, and is organized in seven different subject areas including literature and language; medicine, science, and technology; and religion and philosophy. The collection also includes thousands of important works from the Americas.

The eighteenth century has been called "The Age of Enlightenment." It was a period of rapid advance in print culture and publishing, in world exploration, and in the rapid growth of science and technology – all of which had a profound impact on the political and cultural landscape. At the end of the century the American Revolution, French Revolution and Industrial Revolution, perhaps three of the most significant events in modern history, set in motion developments that eventually dominated world political, economic, and social life.

In a groundbreaking effort, Gale initiated a revolution of its own: digitization of epic proportions to preserve these invaluable works in the largest online archive of its kind. Contributions from major world libraries constitute over 175,000 original printed works. Scanned images of the actual pages, rather than transcriptions, recreate the works *as they first appeared.*

Now for the first time, these high-quality digital scans of original works are available via print-on-demand, making them readily accessible to libraries, students, independent scholars, and readers of all ages.

For our initial release we have created seven robust collections to form one the world's most comprehensive catalogs of 18th century works.

Initial Gale ECCO Print Editions collections include:

History and Geography
Rich in titles on English life and social history, this collection spans the world as it was known to eighteenth-century historians and explorers. Titles include a wealth of travel accounts and diaries, histories of nations from throughout the world, and maps and charts of a world that was still being discovered. Students of the War of American Independence will find fascinating accounts from the British side of conflict.

Social Science
Delve into what it was like to live during the eighteenth century by reading the first-hand accounts of everyday people, including city dwellers and farmers, businessmen and bankers, artisans and merchants, artists and their patrons, politicians and their constituents. Original texts make the American, French, and Industrial revolutions vividly contemporary.

Medicine, Science and Technology
Medical theory and practice of the 1700s developed rapidly, as is evidenced by the extensive collection, which includes descriptions of diseases, their conditions, and treatments. Books on science and technology, agriculture, military technology, natural philosophy, even cookbooks, are all contained here.

Literature and Language
Western literary study flows out of eighteenth-century works by Alexander Pope, Daniel Defoe, Henry Fielding, Frances Burney, Denis Diderot, Johann Gottfried Herder, Johann Wolfgang von Goethe, and others. Experience the birth of the modern novel, or compare the development of language using dictionaries and grammar discourses.

Religion and Philosophy
The Age of Enlightenment profoundly enriched religious and philosophical understanding and continues to influence present-day thinking. Works collected here include masterpieces by David Hume, Immanuel Kant, and Jean-Jacques Rousseau, as well as religious sermons and moral debates on the issues of the day, such as the slave trade. The Age of Reason saw conflict between Protestantism and Catholicism transformed into one between faith and logic -- a debate that continues in the twenty-first century.

Law and Reference
This collection reveals the history of English common law and Empire law in a vastly changing world of British expansion. Dominating the legal field is the *Commentaries of the Law of England* by Sir William Blackstone, which first appeared in 1765. Reference works such as almanacs and catalogues continue to educate us by revealing the day-to-day workings of society.

Fine Arts
The eighteenth-century fascination with Greek and Roman antiquity followed the systematic excavation of the ruins at Pompeii and Herculaneum in southern Italy; and after 1750 a neoclassical style dominated all artistic fields. The titles here trace developments in mostly English-language works on painting, sculpture, architecture, music, theater, and other disciplines. Instructional works on musical instruments, catalogs of art objects, comic operas, and more are also included.

The BiblioLife Network

This project was made possible in part by the BiblioLife Network (BLN), a project aimed at addressing some of the huge challenges facing book preservationists around the world. The BLN includes libraries, library networks, archives, subject matter experts, online communities and library service providers. We believe every book ever published should be available as a high-quality print reproduction; printed on-demand anywhere in the world. This insures the ongoing accessibility of the content and helps generate sustainable revenue for the libraries and organizations that work to preserve these important materials.

The following book is in the "public domain" and represents an authentic reproduction of the text as printed by the original publisher. While we have attempted to accurately maintain the integrity of the original work, there are sometimes problems with the original work or the micro-film from which the books were digitized. This can result in minor errors in reproduction. Possible imperfections include missing and blurred pages, poor pictures, markings and other reproduction issues beyond our control. Because this work is culturally important, we have made it available as part of our commitment to protecting, preserving, and promoting the world's literature.

GUIDE TO FOLD-OUTS MAPS and OVERSIZED IMAGES

The book you are reading was digitized from microfilm captured over the past thirty to forty years. Years after the creation of the original microfilm, the book was converted to digital files and made available in an online database.

In an online database, page images do not need to conform to the size restrictions found in a printed book. When converting these images back into a printed bound book, the page sizes are standardized in ways that maintain the detail of the original. For large images, such as fold-out maps, the original page image is split into two or more pages

Guidelines used to determine how to split the page image follows:

• Some images are split vertically; large images require vertical and horizontal splits.
• For horizontal splits, the content is split left to right.
• For vertical splits, the content is split from top to bottom.
• For both vertical and horizontal splits, the image is processed from top left to bottom right.

Nº IX.

SKETCHES

OF THE

HISTORY AND ANTIQUITIES

OF THE PARISH OF

STOKE NEWINGTON,

IN THE COUNTY OF

MIDDLESEX.

NEWINGTON.

NEWINGTON, or STOKE* NEWINGTON, for it is called by both names, and in old records *Neutone, Newton*, and *Neweton Canonicorum*, is a small parish, out of the bills of mortality, about three miles north of London, on the east side of Finsbury division of the hundred of Ossulston, in the county of Middlesex; and is bounded by the parishes of Hornsey, Islington, Hackney †, and Tottenham.

It is supposed to contain about 545 acres of land, and is assessed to the land-tax 482*l*. 1*s*. 6*d*. The window-tax at present produces 347*l*. 7*s*. 6*d*. The house-tax from April 5, 1782, to April 5, 1783, amounts to 173*l*. 12*s*. 6*d*. The highway assessment or compositions for statute duty, from Michaelmas 1781, to Michaelmas 1782, amount to 123*l*. 11*s*. 6*d*. It contains one parish church, two dissenting meeting houses, one in Church Street, the other at Newington Green, and about 195 houses, in which there are one family of Jews, five or six of Quakers, one of Catholicks, and about 40 of other Dissenters.

Newington sends six men to the Eastern battalion of the Middlesex militia; and a resolution having been come to in the summer of 1781, for the parish to provide substitutes for those who might be chosen by lot to serve, upon the payment of five shil-

---

* Perhaps it had the adjunct of *Stoke* from its situation formerly among woods, Saxon Stoc (as is the case with many other places in the kingdom); there having been so lately as in 1649 no less than 77 acres and 20 poles of wood land in the demesne only.

† Strype says, " one ward of Hackney is called Stoke Newington, and lies on " the West side of the great Northern road; on the West side of which road is the " parish of Stoke Newington and Newington Green." Survey of London, B. VI. p. 131. Q. Is not this an inaccurate description? The houses on the East side of the road, commonly supposed to be in Newington, are really in Hackney parish.

lings *per* man; the number of persons who took the benefit thereof in the course of the year was 59, whence an idea may be formed of the number of *fighting men* the parish is able to raise.

The land lies in general much on a level; some of it is arable, but the greater part meadow or pasture; the soil on the south side of the parish pretty much gravel, on the North clay; many of the fields watered by the windings of the New River, which is a great convenience to the inhabitants, as well as ornament to the parish.

The great road from London to Hertford and Cambridge, which in its passage through the village separates the parishes of Newington and Hackney, and Finsbury and Tower divisions of Ossulston hundred, is delineated in the county maps as the ancient "Ermen street, which is corrupted from the Saxon name of a "Roman road, that was, according to Somner, written Herman, "*Here* in that language signifying an army, and *Hereman* a sol- "dier, which is no more than Via Militaris*." It led from Newhaven on the coast of Sussex through Surrey to London, and thence passing under Cripplegate†, through the counties of Middlesex, Hertford, Essex, Cambridge, Suffolk, and Norfolk, to *Venta Icenorum*, now Castor, a little to the South of Norwich: but I drew it in my own mind along a green lane in this neighbourhood, with which I am well acquainted; and by the account which Mr. Salmon gives of it‡, I am in the main confirmed in my idea as to its course through this and the neighbouring parishes. I apprehend that it leaves the great road on the east by Kingsland Green a little to the north of the turnpike, in the parish of Hackney; passes along that parish, then separates the parishes of Hornsey and Islington, afterwards of Newington and Islington on the North side of Newington Green, again of Hornsey and Islington, and again of Newington and Islington, and then of Newington and

---

* Salmon's History of Hertfordshire, art. *Cheshunt*.
† According to the System of Geography, art. *London*. ‡ Loc. citat.

STOKE NEWINGTON.

Hornsey as far as the end of the hundred; it then, I believe, separates the parishes of Tottenham and Hornsey, and the hundreds of Edmonton and Ossulston, till it reaches about as far as the green lane turnpike, when it enters the parish of Tottenham, passes through the hamlets of Wood Green and Bowes Farm, and thence into the parish of Edmonton to the entrance of Palmer's Green, and between that hamlet and some land which is the property of Stephen Peter Godin, esq. of Southgate, by a house formerly in the possession of Mr. Justice Birch, into the road leading from Tanner's End, Edmonton, to the north part of Southgate. Between Newington Green and Palmer's Green the New River crosses it seven times.

The manor and the parish are co-extensive. The manor and the patronage of the rectory are the property of the prebendary of Newington, one of the prebends of St. Paul's cathedral, to which they belonged from the Conquest. In Domesday survey the canons of St. Pauls held 2 hides 2 carucates and a half. There were 4 villans and 37 cottagers on 10 acres. This land (then valued at 41*s.*) was worth 40*s.* in the time of king Edward the Confessor. It was then and since in the demesne of St. Paul*.

This manor, together with about 325 acres of land therein, is the corps of the prebend, which is in the gift of the lord bishop of London, who collates to it.

The prebendary has the sixteenth stall on the left side of the choir in St. Paul's cathedral. He pays to the king 28*l.* for first fruits, and to the bishop of London 2*l.* 16*s.* yearly tithes.

---

* In Neutone hnt canonici S Pauli II. hid. Ad. II.
car 7 dim̃ est ibi tra. 7 ĩh sunt. Ibi. IIII. uilli. 7 XXXVII.
cot de. X. acr. H tra ual. XL. 1. sol. qdo recep similir.
T.R.E. XL. sol. Hæc jacuit 7 jacet in dño S Pauli.

  Domesday, fol. 128, a. col. 1. omitted in Dugdale's Extracts from
   Domesday at the end of his History of St. Paul's.

The church is a rectory in the archdeaconry of Middlesex, and diocese of London, but under the peculiar jurisdiction of the dean and chapter of St. Paul's, subject neither to bishop nor archdeacon, saving only when the bishop visits *tam in capite, quam in membris*. The prebendary is patron in right of his prebend; and the clerk to whom he gives it is instituted and admitted by the dean and chapter, and their commissary issues the mandate for induction. The rector pays 10*l.* for first fruits, and 1*l.* yearly tithes to the king, and 6*s.* 8*d.* procuration to the dean and chapter.

Here is a parsonage house, and a glebe of 18 acres and a half, which are the rector's freehold, all the rest of the parish being either copyhold or leasehold.

PREBENDARIES.

GILBERT FOLIOT, before 1139; bishop of Hereford 1148; of London 1163, where he died 1187.

JOHN DE GARLAND.

WILLIAM COMIN.

RANULF DE BISACIA, canon of St. Paul's 1217—1243.

JOHN DE RAMESEY.

HENRY DE WENGHAM, chamberlain of Gascony 1252; dean of Totenhale and of St. Martin, London, 1255; and also high chancellor of England; elected bishop of Winchester 1259, which he refused, fearing the king his patron's displeasure; but about the end of the year was chosen bishop of London, and died 1261 or 2.

HENRY DE WENGHAM, archdeacon of Middlesex, and executor to his name-sake the bishop just mentioned; from 1262 to 1266, and perhaps afterwards.

THOMAS DE INGALDESTHORP, rector of Pagham, in the diocese of Chichester; archdeacon of Sudbury, 1267; archdeacon of

Middlesex, and dean of St. Paul's, 1276; bishop of Rochester, 1283, where he died and was buried 1291.

RALPH DE BAUDAKE, or BALDOCK, educated at Merton College, prebendary of Holborn before 1271, and of Isledon (hod. Islington); archdeacon of London, and 1294 dean; and in 1300 bishop of London, where he died and was buried 1313. He was chancellor of England, but resigned within a year.

JOHN DE EVERDON, baron of the Exchequer 1307—1313; resigned Stoke Basset in the diocese of Lincoln 1307; chancellor of the Exchequer, 1308; dean of Wolverhampton, and prebend of Tarleton in Sarum, and of Giveldale in Ripon, 1311; dean of London, 1328, where he died and was buried 1336.

ROGER DE STRATHONE, succeeded 1314 by

JOHN DE SANDALE, chaplain to Edward II. and chancellor of the Exchequer 1307; rector of Wimbleton, and of Dunbar in Scotland, 1309, holding at the same time the churches of Simondesburn, in the diocese of Dublin; Mims and Wymbish, in the diocese of London; chancellor of the church of Dublin, and a prebendary of Wells; treasurer of Litchfield 1311; master of the hospital of St. Katharine, 1312*; rector of Solehull 1313; prebendary of Finglas, Dublin; locum tenens of the king's treasury, and 1313 treasurer; canon of York 1314; chancellor of England, and prebendary of Exeter 1315; bishop of Winchester 1316; and dying 1319, was buried in St. Mary Overy's church.

ROGER DE NORTHBURGH had this prebend granted him by king Edward II. the see of London being void, Jan. 1, 1316 or 1317; also the archdeaconry of Richmond, and a prebend of Hereford; in 1322 he was made bishop of Coventry and Litchfield. He was lord keeper and lord treasurer; and died in November or December 1359.

THOMAS DE LYNTON, dean of his majesty's chapel, had this prebend granted him by king Richard II. Nov. 12, 1381.

* 1315. History of that Hospital, p. 81.

JOHN

JOHN BARNET, ratified in this prebend by the king, Nov. 30, 1387.

THOMAS MORE, or MOOR, collated by the bishop of London, June 6, 1391. He was prebend of Salisbury 1389; archdeacon of Colchester 1398; and dean of London 1416. He died Dec. 23, 1421.

JOHN LANGTON, chancellor of the university of Cambridge, and master of Pembroke Hall, collated Nov. or Dec. 9, 1428; made bishop of St. David's in 1446.

WILLIAM BRIGGEFORD, vicar of Braughing, which he resigned 1428; rector of Hadham 1438; prebendary of Isledon 1442; resigned for this, April 15, 1447.

WILLIAM SAY, D. D. prebendary of Isledon 1447; dean of St. Paul's 1457; resigned this prebend 1464 for that of Wenlakesbarn.

JOHN CHADWORTH, rector of Stepney after 1450; prebend of Wenlakesbarn 1462; collated to this prebend July 18, 1464; vicar of Fulham 1467; died before August 6, 1471. Mr. Newcourt does not think him the same with the bishop of Lincoln 1452, archdeacon of Wilts 1459, and provost of King's college, Cambridge.

The Hon. WILLIAM DUDLEY, M. A. third son of John Sutton, alias Dudley, lord Dudley, rector of Hindon 1466; prebend of Cadington 1468; dean of the king's chapel, and canon of Wells; collated to this prebend Aug. 15, 1471, resigned about February 1472; dean of Windsor Dec. 4, 1473; archdeacon of Middlesex Nov. 16, 1475; bishop of Durham Oct. 1476; died 1483, and buried in St. Nicholas' chapel, Westminster, where he has a brass.

RICHARD LICHFIELD, LL. D. Feb. 20, 1472; prebend of Cadington and Wenlakesbarn, rector of Stepney, and archdeacon of Middlesex and Bath; died Feb. 27, 1496; buried in St. Paul's.

HUGH OLDHAM, of Exeter college, Oxford, and Queen's college, Cambridge, rector of St. Mildred, Bread Street, 1485—1488,

and

and Cheshunt 1494; prebend of Sarum 1495; collated to this prebend March 11, 1496; prebend of York 1499; canon of Lincoln; founder of Manchester school; made bishop of Exeter in 1504; died June 25, 1519.

JOHN PICKERING, B. D. He had the prebend in St. Paul's church *consumpt. per mare*, 1494, which he resigned for this Jan. 6, 1504; died in 1511.

JOHN YOUNG, LL. D. rector of St. Stephen, Walbroke, 1502; St. Mary le Bow 1504; master of the Rolls 1507; prebend of Holbourn 1511; collated to this prebend Feb. 10 or 11, 1511; rector of St. Magnus, London, 1514; dean of York, May 17, 1514; died April 25, 1516, and buried at the Rolls, where his monument remains.

THOMAS WELLS, D. D. a benefactor to New College, Oxford, April 29, 1516; rector of Harlington 1505; St. Leonard's Eastcheap 1513, and of Heyford Warine, co. Oxon.

WILLIAM WARHAM, archdeacon of Canbury; rector of Harrow Oct. 14, 1532—1537, and of Hayes; died before 1557.

JOHN BOXHALL, D. D. secretary of state to queen Mary, archdeacon of Ely, prebendary of Winchester, warden of Winchester college, 1554; dean of Peterborough, Norwich, and Windsor, 1557; prebendary of York and Salisbury; collated to this prebend May 14, 1558; deprived by queen Elizabeth; died 1570.

THOMAS PENNY, M. A. March 2, 1559; deprived.

ROBERT KING, M. A. Dec. 3, 1577; rector of Orset, Essex, 1579; died 1584.

HUGH LLOYD, LL. B. a most admired grammarian, chancellor of the diocese of Rochester 1578, and chief master of Winchester school; collated to this prebend Nov. 12, 1584; died Oct. 17, 1601, and was buried in New college outer chapel, Oxford.

ZACHARIAH PASFIELD, D. D. rector of East Haningfield, Essex, 1600; collated to this prebend Oct. 24, 1601; vicar of Asheldam 1604; dean and rector of Bocking in Essex, 1609; died before Dec. 5, 1616.

RICHARD

RICHARD CLUET, D. D. archdeacon of Middlesex, vicar of Fulham, rector of St. Anne, Aldersgate, 1607; sequestered for his loyalty 1642; resigned.

WILLIAM PRICHARD, M. A. June 13, 1620; died.

THOMAS TURNER, D. D. April 14, 1629; domestic chaplain to William Laud, archbishop of Canterbury; chaplain in ordinary to king Charles; chancellor of St. Paul's cathedral, Oct. 29, 1629; and 1633 canon residentiary; dean of Rochester 1641, and of Canterbury 1643. He suffered greatly during the Usurpation, and lost his spiritualities for his loyalty, but enjoyed them again after the Restoration. He died Oct. 8, 1672, aged about 81, and was buried in the cathedral of Canterbury.

EDWARD STILLINGFLEET, D. D. of St. John's College, Cambridge, rector of St. Andrew, Holborn; archdeacon of London, May 4, 1677; dean of St. Paul's, Oct. 11, 1672; made bishop of Worcester in October 1689; died March 27, 1699.

JOHN TILLOTSON, D. D. of Clare Hall, Cambridge, preacher at Lincoln's Inn; dean of St. Paul's, Dec. 24, 1689; made archbishop of Canterbury May 28, 1691; died Nov. 22, 1694.

JOHN HUNT, B. D. June 19, 1691.

JOHN MILLINGTON, D. D. vicar of Kensington, and rector of Stoke Newington; buried at Newington April 26, 1728.

JOSEPH SMITH, D. D. provost of Queen's College, Oxford, 1728; died Nov. 23, 1756.

Dr. SAMUEL NICOLLS, rector of St. James's, Westminster, and of Northall; master of the Temple; died Nov. 18, 1763.

CHARLES WESTON, M. A. prebendary of Durham, and rector of Therfield, in Hertfordshire.

The church is dedicated to St. *Mary*; the tower at the West end contains five bells. It has been twice enlarged; first in 1716, when it was nearly doubled in point of size, by taking in about 20 feet in breadth and 44 in length of the North side of the church-yard, in order to erect about 24 pews; and secondly in 1723, by taking in about 10 feet in depth and 22 in breadth of the East part of the church-yard, in order to enlarge the chancel.

In the chancel is a handsome monument fixed against the South wall, consisting of pillars of different marbles, forming two compartments, in one of which kneels a gentleman with a helmet behind him, and in the other facing him a lady with a daughter behind her; over him is inscribed

   Obiit 29° Decembris, Anno Domini 1580.

Under him is the following inscription:

  Vivo miles, enim Christo ductore triumpho,
   Stix, caro, mors, mundus, cuncta subacta mihi.
  Exivi terris fessus velut histrio scena,
   Acta est ætatis fabula longa meæ.
  Finis adest, clare, spectantes plaudite, vixi,
   Et cum desisto vivere, vivo magis.

Under her the following:

  Vivo, sed absque meo mors est mea vita marito,
   Cumque viro veris sum viduata bonis.
  Charus eras summis, imisque benignus, at uni
   O mihi quam charus quamque benignus eras!
  Rara fuit pietas genus et tibi nobile: Vixi:
   Tu cum desistis vivere, vivo minus.

Lower on the base (but now invisible, two pews having been erected before it) is the following:

  Vivo prius durus mutusque, sed undique mutor,
   Ore loquax, mollis pectore fio lapis.
  Me tua mollivit (mi Dudlei) vivida virtus:
   Quæ tam sancta fuit vita perennis erit.
  Et quæ freta viro optato simul optima vixti,
   Tu (neque desistis vivere) vivis adhuc.

At the top of all in the centre is a coat of arms, with four grand quarters quarterly; firſt grand quarter, 1. Or, a lion rampant double tailed Vert, langued Gules, charged with a creſcent of the field for difference; *Duddeleye*. 2. Gules, a Cinquefoil ermine, a creſcent Or, for difference; *Bellomont*. 3. Or, 2 lions paſſant Azure, langued Gules; *Somery*. 4. Argent, a croſs moline Azure; I fancy *Lexington*. In the center of this grand quarter a creſcent Sable for difference. Second grand quarter; 1 and 4. Argent, a Maunch Gules; 2 and 3. Sable, a bend flory and counterflory Or. Third grand quarter, 1. Barry of 6, Or and Azure, on a canton Gules a Croſs Croſlet of the firſt; 2. quarterly Or and Gules, a Bordure vaire; 3. Or, a croſs Sable; 4. Vert, 3 Lioncels rampant Argent (at leaſt I think they ſeem to have been deſigned for ſuch) langued Gules, crowned, collared, and a chain paſſing between their fore legs, all Or. Fourth grand quarter as the firſt; a creſcent Gules for difference in the center of the whole. At the top a helmet, thereon an ancient ducal coronet, in which is a creſt, a lion's head and neck Azure, langued Gules, charged on the breaſt with a creſcent Or for difference.

This is the monument of JOHN DUDDELEYE, eſq. ſometime lord of the manor, and his widow ELIZABETH, daughter of John Gardiner, of Grove Place, in the pariſh of Chalfont St. Giles's, in Bucks, eſq. who was buried here June 17, 1602, being then the wife of Thomas Sutton, eſq. founder of the Charter Houſe, to whom ſhe had been married 20 years*; but there is no name on the monument, except in the third line of the third inſcription, as above; nor does the daughter appear to have been buried here.

The baſe is divided into three compartments, of which the center is larger than the other two, and contains the inſcription, but is not to be ſeen but by removing the pews.

* See Bearcroft's Hiſtory of the Charterhouſe, p. 16.

STOKE NEWINGTON.

Against the East wall of the church is a neat plain monument of grey marble, on the top of which is a coat of arms, quarterly, 1. Argent, a bend of lozenges Sable. 2. Ermine, on a chevron Sable 3 crosses Argent. 3. Argent, on a fess, between 3 Azure, 3 birds, perhaps pigeons, of the field. Fourth as the first, in the center a crescent Gules for difference:

> JOHANNES TAVERNER, natus in comitatu Hertfordiensi, familia honesta, parentibus piis et probis. A prima infantia literis operam dedit; primo sub privato magistro; dein Westmonasterii institutus, Cantabrigiæ studuit per annos 8, ubi item Magisterii gradum suscepit. Dein Oxonii per annos 5. Posteaque Johanni King Epo Lon a libellis per annos 9. et unus Prælectorum in collegio Gresham, Lon, per annos 28. Demumq̃ sacris ordinibus susceptis, vicarius de Tillingham in com' Essex, an. 5. Et postremum hujus ecclesiæ rector an. 9. Hic expleto curriculo subtus sepultus fœlicem resurrectionem sperat. Nat. anno 1584. Denatus anno 1638. Vitam duxit cœlibem.
>
>   Vixi, nec quicquam vel vitæ nomine dignum
>   Sensi, vel quare longa petenda foret.
>
>   Hic situs est qui res divinas calluit, artes
>   Omnes, cui lingua et plurima et una fuit.
>   Qui bene judicio purum solidavit acumen,
>   Famam ultra prudens, ac sine teste pius.
>   Qui potuit citius quam quærere munus obire,
>   Seu quod civilis seu toga docta regit.
>   Mens humilis fuit in sublimi corpore; pectus
>   Sincerum, donans dextera, penna volans.
>   Pulcher erat primo, cum vir virtute venustus,
>   In sene mors vixit, dormit is, illa fuit.
>
>   Dies mei velociores [*].

In the South aile upon the ground is a stone, on which is a coat of arms impaled; the baron seems to bear two bars, and

---

[*] Sir Henry Chauncey, and after him Mr. Salmon, in their Histories of Hertfordshire, place this epitaph in Hexton church in that county, where his father had an estate and monument, together with his wife. Professor Ward accounts for this mistake, which perplexed Newcourt, who from it imagined him *vicar* of Hexton, though called *rector* in the epitaph, by supposing Sir Henry copied all the Taverner inscriptions from a pedigree by one of the family. Gresh. Prof. 216.

over all a bend goboné (but this coat and the inscription are very much defaced); the femme bears three pickaxes.

> Deceased Septemb. Anno Domini 1652.
> Here was interred the body of JOHN LEIGH, gent. son of John Leigh, of Leigh Hall, in the county of Lancaster, gent. who was married to Talbot, daughter of Benjamin Pigott, of Gravehurst, in the county of Bedford, esq. By her direction this monument was made.

This gentleman appears by the register to have been buried September 24.

Near to this another; at the top a coat of arms impaled; the baron a chevron between 2 mullets in chief, and a stork in base; the femme a lion rampant; crest, on a wreath a stork.

> M. S.
> V. R. SAMUELIS WRIGHT*, S. T. P.
> Qui agro Eboracensi ortus,
> ac disciplinis liberalibus bene institutus,
> sacrum suum munus rure suscepit,
> deinde Londinum profectus,
> brevi temporis spatio ita se probavit,
> ut ecclesiæ Presbyterianæ pastor eligeretur,
> cui per annos octo & triginta
> pari diligentia & fœlicitate præfuit,
> multigenæ autem doctrinæ
> eas naturæ dotes habuit adjunctas,
> ut in sacris administrandis,
> (quæ summo decore semper præstabat,)
> mentes auditorum attentas reddere,
> sibique facile conciliare posset;
> ad recondita etiam sacrarum literarum
> sensa eruenda
> eximia facultate præditus erat,
> vitæque Christianæ virtutibus conspicuus.
> At defessus tandem labore
> acerbisque doloribus quos fortiter pertulit,
> corpus hic sepeliri jubens,
> in Christo placide obdormivit,
> non. April. A.D. 1746,
> æt. suæ 64.
> *Beati qui in Domino moriuntur.*

Over this tomb-stone hangs a handsome brass chandelier, inscribed, "The gift of Edward Alanson to the parish church of St. "Mary Stoke Newington, 1717."

In this aile also is an ancient flat stone, which has had two large effigies and an inscription to each, and two small effigies; but they are all torn away except one of the small effigies, which is very much defaced.

---

* Of this eminent Dissenting minister a particular account shall be given in our Appendix.

Near the West door upon the ground is a stone, on which is a coat of arms impaled; the Baron seems to be a fess lozengy, invected at top, and engrailed at bottom, in chief 3 bells; the Femme seems to be 3 leopards passant guardant in pale, surmounted by a bend charged with 4 mullets, but it is much injured; crest, on a wreath, seems to be a demi squirrel, holding an oak branch in his mouth.

> Under this stone, in a vault, lyeth the body of JAMES PORTER, of Newington Green, gent. who departed this life August 26, 1693, aged 67 years. Here lyeth also the body of ANN PORTER, wife of the said JAMES PORTER, who departed this life Sept. 8, 1693, aged 57 years. Also the body of GEORGE PORTLR, his son, who departed this life May 12, 1678, aged 7 years 11 mo.

The industrious Weever, in his Ancient Funeral Monuments, has recorded one inscription:

> "Hic iacet MATILDA uxor IOHANNIS EKINGTON,
> "quondam cofferarij hospitij domini regis Edw. quarti; que ob. 1473."

And Mr. Strype, in his Addenda to Stow's Survey, after having mentioned several inscriptions that are inserted in this work, has the following: "In the middle aile two ancient flat burial
"stones, with effigies and inscriptions in brass, but torn away.
"Against the North wall, near the East, is an ancient table mo-
"nument, without any inscription; on the side are some shields,
"one bears the three nails of the cross, another the cross, with
"the crown of thorns hanging on it.

"An ancient flat stone, with Saxon capital letters round it,
"hard to be read.

> "JOHN STOCKER, esq. buried by his fader in S. Thomas chapel in the church of
> "Stoke Newington in Middlesex, by his will dat. Sept. 13, 1500, gives several
> "lands in Newington and Crepulgate *."

* Newington, Reg. Lond.

Every

Every vestige of these is totally lost, except that it is supposed that the "lands in Newington" above-mentioned are those six acres, on part of which the hamlet of the *Palatine* houses now stands.

In the North-West part of the church-yard is a square piece of ground inclosed with iron rails, in the center of which grows a fine yew tree. There is no stone nor any other memorial, but a plate inserted in the West side of the railing, whereon is a coat of arms, quarterly, first and fourth a chevron between 3 leopards faces; second and third, 3 cinquefoils, and underneath "J. F. 1715." This contains the remains of John Farrington, esq. buried here Jan. 25, 1714-15.

Near the North East corner of the church are two monuments inclosed within one railing, on which is the following arms, a lion rampant within a bordure; crest, on a wreath, a demi griffin.

> H. S. E. Quod mortale fuit Samuelis Lane, civis Londinensis, nati apud Coworth, de parochia Vindesorii Antiquioris in Bercheria. Obiit Februarii 27mo, 1708. *Mollis ut herba resurgam.*
>
> Here lyeth the body of Anne Manship, sister to Samuel Lane, who departed this life July 18, 1734, aged 73 years.
>
> Here lyeth the body of John Manship, esq. merchant of London, who departed this life Feb 2, 1749, aged 54 years.

On the East side of the church-yard a monument has lately been erected, on the top of which is this inscription:

> Near this place lyeth the body of Mr. William Pickett, formerly of this parish, who died Feb. 19, 1745, aged 43 years: Also Ann his wife, who died March 22, 1750, aged 42 years: And likewise William, Thomas, and Tabitha, children of the above, who died in their infancy.

This tomb was erected by WILLIAM PICKETT, of London, Goldsmith*, only surviving offspring of the above WILLIAM and ANN, on the melancholy death of his daughter ELIZABETH: And also in memory of five other children, viz. THOMAS, THOMAS, ANN, EDWARD, and GEORGE, who died in their infancy.

On the South side,

A testimony of respect from greatly afflicted parents· In memory of ELIZABETH PICKETT, spinster, who died Dec. 11, 1781, aged 23 years.

At the West end,

This much-lamented young person expired in consequence of her cloaths taking fire the preceding evening.

Lower, on the base,

Reader, if ever you should witness such an affecting scene, recollect that the only method to extinguish the flame, is to stifle it by an immediate covering.

On the North side,

So unaffected, so compos'd a mind,
So firm, yet soft, so strong, yet so refin'd,
Heaven, as pure gold, by flaming tortures tried;
The angel bore them, but the mortal died.

At the East end,

Not a sparrow falls on the ground without our Heavenly Father.

Opposite the North East corner of the church is a tomb-stone, which is the only distinctive memorial here of any person professing the Roman Catholic faith.

In spe resurgendi, et fide Catholica. Here lieth ELIZABETH (AUBREY) CASSILLS, wife of ROBERT CASSILLS; obiit March 24, Anno Dom. 1723-4, ætat. ✠ 47.

* Elected alderman of Cornhill ward in May 1782.

The following is a lift of the Rectors of this parifh, fo far as I was able to recover them.

GODFREY BECKE, buried Jan. 20, 1567-8.

EDWARD SYMPSON was here in October 1574.

JOHN DODD appears to have been here from July 1579 to May 1585.

ROBERT WHITWORTH, married to "Marie Dodd, widow," (probably of his predeceffor) May 14, 1586; buried Aug. 1, 1593.

RICHARD LHOYD entered circa Feb. 3, 1593-4. He was a legatee of 13*l.* 6*s.* 8*d.* under the will of Thomas Sutton, efq. and one of the witneffes to a codicil made by that gentleman on the day of his death; buried April 30, 1629.

JOHN TAVERNER, M. A. buried Aug. 25, 1638. See his monument in the church, p. 11.

WILLIAM HEATH, B. D. fequeftered for his loyalty foon after Dec. 6, 1644 *.

---

* I cannot better illuftrate this gentleman's remarkable attention, and his fucceffor's remarkable inattention to the parifh regifters, than by giving the two following entries, which I have copied *verbatim & literatim ufque ad erratum*; and from the language of the latter it is eafy to infer who was the regiftrar.

"Guilielmus filius natu maximus Guilielmi Heath, hujus ecclïæ rectoris, natus fuit octavo die menfis Augufti anno Dom. 1639: Baptizatus autem die dominico, viz. decimo octavo die menfis prædict' annoq' Domini prædicto, 1639."

"A child unbaptized of my Mr. Manton's, minifter of this parrifh, was burjed June 17, in the year of our Lord God, 1653."

And here by the way I cannot help obferving, that it is furely unreafonable to infert in the fame catalogue the names of minifters who were ejected out of livings that had been fequeftered, and of others who were ejected in confequence of their non-compliance with the requirements of the act of Uniformity. Certainly there is no comparifon between the fituation of a man who (having been inftituted to a benefice in confequence of the ejection of one who was legally in poffeffion, and who, however unworthy he might be in point of incapacity, neglect, or the like, was ejected by an illegal, ufurped power) is himfelf ejected upon the overthrow of that power, and the eftablifhment of legal authority; and of a man, who being in the legal poffeffion of a benefice, pleads that he cannot in confcience comply with the requifitions of an *ex poft facto* law, fuperinducing a qualification which was not required at the time of his inftitution, but is now made a *fine qua non* of his continuing in poffeffion, and therefore voluntarily refigns his living.

THOMAS

THOMAS MANTON, D. D. *of Wadham College, Oxford, one of Cromwell's chaplains, presented by colonel Alexander Popham, the lessee of the manor (supported probably by the* vox populi*), the prebendary being now stripped of his rights by the parliament. He was presented by William earl of Bedford to the rectory of St. Paul, Covent-Garden, in the room of the Rev. Obadiah Sedgwick, probably in* 1756 *or* 7, *when he resigned this living. From Covent Garden he was ejected by the act of uniformity, which took place August* 24, 1662, *and became a most voluminous writer, and a principal leader among the Nonconformist ministers. He died Oct.* 18, 1677, *and was buried here.*

―――― BULL, *presented by a similar usurped authority. Upon the Restoration of king Charles* II. *and the constitution, he was driven out to make way for the restoration of the legal incumbent,*

WILLIAM HEATH, B. D. who resigned in 1664.

SIDRACH SIMPSON, D. D. succeeded Jan. 3, 1664. His name appears as a writer in the Ecclesiastical Controversies of his day; buried Nov. 9, 1704.

JOHN MILLINGTON, D. D. prebendary of this place, and vicar of Kensington; inducted in May 1705. He was buried April 26, 1728.

RALPH THORESBY, M. A. (son of the celebrated antiquary Mr. Ralph Thoresby, author of the " Ducatus Leodiensis," " Vicaria Leodiensis," &c.) presented by Dr. Edmund Gibson, lord bishop of London; died April 24, 1763.

WILLIAM HENRY NICOLLS (son of the Rev. Dr. John Nicolls, vicar of St. Giles, Cripplegate, and rector of St. Luke, Middlesex, and nephew to the prebendary); died July 15, 1767.

WILLIAM COOKE, D. D. fellow of Eton College, rector of Denham in the county of Bucks; provost of King's College, Cambridge about March 1772, elected vice chancellor of the university Oct. 12, 1772; prebendary of Ely about April 1780, and dean in July 1780.

The first election of a Lecturer I apprehend to have been on Jan. 30, 1704-5, in the person of

The Rev. RICHARD SEAR, rector of Hornsey, and of St. Alban, Wood Street; buried here Feb. 24, 1742-3.

RALPH THORESBY, M. A. the rector, died April 24, 1763.

JOHN DEERE THOMAS, resigned about 1769.

RICHARD CLARKE, M. A. author of an Essay on the Number Seven, and other mystical works; resigned at Christmas 1776.

NICHOLAS GRIFFINHOOFE, B. D. rector 1749 of Woodham Mortimer, and 1761 Stow Mary's, in Essex, elected lecturer of this parish Jan. 13, 1777.

Ministers of the Dissenting Meeting-house at Newington.

The Rev. JOSEPH CAWTHORNE, minister, before the act of Uniformity, of one of the churches in Stamford, Lincolnshire; buried here March 8, 1706-7.

...... EATON.

MARTIN TOMKINS, brother to Mr. Hardinge Tomkins, clerk to the company of Fishmongers, London; resigned.

JOHN HILL, minister here in 1734; resigned, upon being chose to succeed Dr. Ridgley, a Dissenting minister in London.

SAMUEL SNASHALL: resigned.

MEREDITH TOWNSEND, April 1752.

In a collection of "Fifty Views of Villages, &c. drawn by "the celebrated M. Chatelaine," and engraved by J. Roberts in 1731, is "The North West View of Newington," and "The "South West View of Newington Church." Both these, by the favour of Messrs. Sayer and Bennett, who have lent the original plates, are given in the present History.

Mr.

The North West View of Newington.

The South West View of Newington Church.

STOKE NEWINGTON.

Mr. Snelling mentions Stoke Newington among the towns whence tradesmens tokens were issued in the last century. We have not been able to meet with any that can certainly be ascertained to belong to it. Mr. Tutet's collection has one, with the name of "Laurence Short, Adam and Eve, Newington, $^S_{L.E.}$" which more probably belongs to Newington Butts, in Surrey. One, however, is here engraved from the same collection, which, if not issued at Stoke Newington, was without doubt there circulated, being the token of " John Ball, at the Boarded House " neere Newington Green." This was a house of entertainment, the sign of The Salutation, at Ball's Pond, a little hamlet in the parish of Islington, near Newington Green. Stoke Newington has very little interest in Newington Green, including only part of the North side, containing 11 houses and the meeting house.

The first lay lord of the manor that I know any thing of, was WILLIAM PATTEN, esq. one of the four tellers of the receipt of the queen's exchequer at Westminster, receiver-general of her highness's revenues within the county of York, customer of London outward, and one of her highness's justices of the peace within the county of Middlesex, who held this manor by lease from Thomas Penny, clerk, prebend of St. Paul's, London, bearing date April 16, 1565, for 99 years, to commence from Michaelmas 1576. Mr. Patten was grandson to Richard Patten, of Bollow, in the county of Derby, the direct ancestor by a younger son of the family of Patten*, now of Bank in Warrington, in the county of Lancaster, and brother to William Patten, surnamed of Wainfleet, sometime lord bishop of Winchester, twice lord chancellor of England, and founder of Magdalen College, Oxon. This gentleman in 1563, to use the words of honest John Stow, "repaired, or rather new builded, the parish church," including a chapel (the property of the lord of the manor), which is a principal part of the ancient edifice. Over the principal door is inscribed the date of its erection, with these words, "Ab alto;" over the chapel door, between the letters W. P. are his arms, the blazon of which is as follows: Quarterly, first seems to be

---

* The descent of the present family of Patten from the said Richard clearly appears from the following laconic genealogical epitaph, which I copied in the churchyard of Warrington, in June 1774:

Here lye interred
HUMPHREY PATTEN, son of RICHARD, brother to WILLIAM of Waynflete:
THOMAS PATTEN, his oldest son:
THOMAS PATTEN, his oldest son,
May 30, 1639:
THOMAS PATTEN, his oldest son,
Sept. 8, 1653:
THOMAS PATTEN, his oldest son,
Nov. 25, 1684:
THOMAS PATTEN, his eldest son,
dyed April 2, 1726, aged 63.

Barry

Barry of 5 . . . . . and Ermine, in a canton a cross paté, fitché; but in the books of the College of Arms, in which the other 3 quarters appear, the arms ascribed to him are lozengy Sable and Ermine, a canton Gules, for *Patten*. 2. Azure, on a bend Or, 3 cinquefoils Gules, for *Westingcroft*. 3. Argent, a chevron Gules, between 3 hurts, for *Baskerville*; the name of his mother, who was an heiress. 4. Ermine, a cross moline, Sable, for *Goddard* of Herefordshire, from whom his mother's mother was descended; motto *Prospice*. His eldest son Mercury Patten was in 1603 Bluemantle pursuivant of arms.

The next lord of the manor was the forementioned JOHN DUDDELEYE*, esq. to whom Mr. Patten, 13 Eliz. sold his lease. He was second son of the Hon. Thomas Dudley, of Yeanwith, in the county of Westmoreland, by Sarah his wife, daughter and coheir of Launcelot Thirkeld, of Yeanwith, esq. which Thomas Dudley was seventh son of Edmund Sutton, alias Dudley, lord Dudley†, by Maud his second wife, daughter of Thomas the

---

* Sic in Testamento.

† A distinguished branch of this family (though, having never been able to get a sight of the pedigree of the ancient lords Dudley, I cannot ascertain in what degree of relation he stood) was Edmund Dudley, of famous memory, who, with Sir Richard Empson, was attainted, and beheaded on Tower Hill Aug. 17, 1510. He married Elizabeth, daughter of Edward Grey viscount Lisle, and his eldest son I take to have been John Sutton, alias Dudley, who was restored in blood, and made lord Dudley, viscount Lisle, a knight of the garter, lord high admiral of England, earl of Warwick, and at length duke of Northumberland, but was afterwards also beheaded on Tower Hill Aug. 22, 1553. He married Jane, sole daughter and heiress of the Right Hon. Sir Edward Guildeford, lord-warden of the Cinque Ports, by whom he had issue (*inter alios*) Ambrose, created earl of Warwick; Robert, created earl of Leicester; lord Guildeford Dudley, married to lady Jane Grey, eldest daughter and co-heiress of Henry duke of Suffolk, proclaimed queen of England on the death of king Edward VI. (who were both beheaded on Tower Hill Feb. 12, 1554-5, as the duke her father also was eleven days after); and Mary, who became at length sole heiress of the family, and was married to Sir Henry Sidney, knight of the garter, lord deputy of Ireland, &c. by whom she was mother of the celebrated Sir Philip Sidney, Robert, created earl of Leicester, and Sir Thomas Sidney.

twelfth

twelfth lord Clifford. The said John Dudley married Elizabeth, daughter of John Gardiner, of Grove Place, in the parish of Chalfont St. Giles in Buckinghamshire. Mr. Robert Dudley, alderman of Newcastle-upon-Tyne, to whom Sutton by will leaves a legacy of 30*l.* was his nephew, second son of his elder brother, Richard Dudley, of Yeanwith, esq.

The old mansion-house was, as such houses every where usually were, just by the church, a little to the East of it; and in a house adjoining to the church-yard, which is built upon the site of a part of it, is the following old coat of arms, very well carved in wood, but it has been injured and very much neglected: Quarterly of 16: 1. A Lion rampant (I suppose *Dudley*, though the double tail, the distinctive mark of this family, does not appear here that I remember, but does in the sinister supporter). 2. 2 Lions passant, *Somery*, anciently baron of Dudley. 3. A quaticfoil pierced; this is probably a mistake of the carver, or of me the copyist, and should be a cinquefoil, the arms of *Bellomont*, anciently earl of Leicester. 4. 3 torteaux and a label, all in chief, *Grey*. 5. A cross flory, probably *Lexington*. 6. A manche, *Hastings* earl of Pembroke. 7. Barry, an Orle of martlets, *Valence* earl of Pembroke. 8. Vair, probably *De Ferrars* earl of Derby. 9. 7 Mascles conjoined, 3, 3, 1, *De Quincy* earl of Winchester. 10. 3 Garbes. 11. A Lion rampant. 12. A fess, between 6 cross croslets, 3 and 3, *Beauchamp* earl of Warwick. 13. Cheque, a chevron, perhaps Ermine. 14. A chevron between 10 crosses patée, 6 and 4, *Berkeley* lord Berkeley. 15. A Lion passant gardant crowned; and 16. A fess between 2 chevrons, two coats borne by Sir *John Lisle*, one of the knights of the Garter at the first institution of the order. The whole within a garter. Over an earl's coronet a helmet and wreath, but the crest is broken off. Supporters, the dexter, a Lion rampant guardant, crowned with an earl's coronet; the sinister, a Lion rampant double tailed, gorged with a coronet, thereto a chain affixed, passing between his fore

legs

legs and reflexed over his back; the top of his head is broke, but I fancy he never had a coronet. Motto, on a strait scroll under the coat,

Ung Dieu, ung Roy   Servier ie doy.

This I conceive to be the arms of Ambrose earl of Warwick before mentioned, and might be set up by Mr. Dudley as arms of patronage or alliance; for it does not appear by the registers, or any other authentic document that I know of, that that noble earl, or his brother the earl of Leicester, ever had any interest or property here. There has indeed long been a tradition current in the parish, that the mansion-house was the residence of one of those two noble earls, and that in or about it the princess Elizabeth was secreted during the reign of her sister Mary; and the names of two old gentlemen are mentioned, both living within these 20 years past, of whom one remembered seeing a brick tower, which was probably part of the offices or a pleasure house belonging to the mansion; and the other, a respectable inhabitant of the parish, positively asserted, that a stair-case had been in existence which led up to the identical spot where her highness had been concealed; and it is very possible that if she found it necessary to keep out of sight during the reign of her sister, her friend lord Leicester might think this a convenient place at some times to secure her in; a secluded village, yet at a convenient distance from the metropolis, and in the house of a younger branch of his family, over whom he might have influence, and about which perhaps several private recesses might be found. Thus much is certain, that Mr. Dudley's lady " had the honour " to be well known to, and to have received visits from, the " queen (Elizabeth) in Mr. Dudley her first husband's time, in " one of which her majesty taking a jewel of great value from " her hair, made a present of it to their daughter Miss Ann " Dudley."

"Dudley*." Mr. Dudley died, as appears above, Dec. 29, 1580, leaving his widow "executrix and co-partner in his for-"tunes with their sole child" Anne, born Feb. 12, 1574-5. About the middle of the year 1582 Mrs. Dudley was married to Thomas Sutton, esq. master-general of the ordnance in the North, and afterwards the celebrated founder of the hospital in the Charter House; and he becoming hereby possessed of the moiety of this manor, made it his country seat, and it continued in his possession till the death of his lady, who was buried here in great state June 17, 1602. He died at his house at Hackney, Dec. 12, 1611, aged 79, having by his will bequeathed to the poor of this parish 10*l.* and towards the mending of the highways between Islington and Newington 26*l.* 13*s.* 4*d.*

In 1590 Miss Dudley was married to Francis Popham, esq. afterwards Sir Francis Popham†, knt. son and heir of Sir John Popham, knt. chief justice of the court of King's bench; and upon the death of her mother, I apprehend, all her father's interest here devolved, by bequest, settlement, or purchase, to her said husband, who was buried here Aug. 15, 1644. He was succeeded by his son and heir Alexander Popham, esq. a colonel in the rebel army, who, when the prebendal estate was sequestered, purchased it of the sequestrators, and thus became (not indeed *de jure*, but *de facto & pro tempore*) lord of the manor in fee, till the restoration of the king to his throne, and of the clergy to their rights, when he reverted to his former state of lessee. Some years before the expiration of the lease (I apprehend) he procured from the prebendary a new one for three lives‡, empowering him to take down the manor house, and let the ground whereon it

---

* Dr. Bearcroft's History of Mr. Sutton.

† The arms of Popham were Argent, on a chief Gules 3 bucks heads cabossed Or; crest, a buck's head erased proper.

‡ I acknowledge that I have no certain evidence of this fact, but from several concurring circumstances think it very probable.

stood on building leases, which began about 1667, and in succeeding years a number of houses were built upon the scite of it; the garden was converted into small gardens for the use of those houses, and a terrace walk between rows of lofty elms, which was christened *Queen Elizabeth's Walk*, was carried across the middle of the home field, and left by way of promenade for the inhabitants of those houses; but having never been shut up, it is become a public walk and a passage to the adjacent fields, through which there are paths to Hornsey, Tottenham, &c. An ancient decaying brick portal, which was the East gate of the chateau, and now opens into a neighbouring farm-yard, is the last fading remain of its ancient dignity. At Midsummer 1695 a new lease was given of some of these houses; Alexander Popham, also of Littlecote, in the county of Wilts, esq. being then in possession of the manor during the lives of himself, his lady (Anne, daughter of Ralph duke of Montague, by whom he had issue Elizabeth, sole daughter and heiress, who married first Edward Richard, lord viscount Hinchingbrook; and secondly, Francis Seymour, esq. brother to Edward late duke of Somerset), and his uncle Alexander Popham, esq. In 1699 Mr. Popham sold all his interest here to Thomas Gunston, of this parish, esq. who designing to make this the place of his residence, built himself a handsome house in the manor, but died unmarried when he had just finished it, Nov. 11, 1700, and was buried in the family vault in the chancel*. This event produced the Eulogy upon the house and its builder, which appears in the Appendix to this History.

The manor, as part of the residue of his estate, devolved to his sister Mary, then lately become the second wife of the Right Hon. Sir Thomas Abney, knt. lord mayor of London. He was a younger son of James Abney, of Willesley, in the county of Derby, esq. (son and heir of George Abney, of the same place,

---

* Mr. Gunston bore Or, on a bend Sable 3 stars of 6 points Argent.

esq.) was born in January 1639-40; was elected sheriff of London and Middlesex in 1693, and in the year following alderman of Vintry Ward within the city of London, and received the honour of knighthood; in 1700 was elected lord-mayor, and in 1701 one of the representatives in parliament for the city; he was also a director of the Bank of England from its first institution in 1694, and president of St. Thomas's Hospital. He died senior alderman of the city Feb. 6, 1721-2, and was buried in St. Peter's church, Cornhill*. He bore Ermine, on a cross Sable 5 bezants, with an escutcheon of pretence of Gunston. Upon his death the plenary possession of the manor devolved to his widow, who about 11 years after removed hither with her family, of which the celebrated Isaac Watts, D. D. a learned and pious Dissenting minister, was a member. About the year 1712, in consequence of those "Wearisome Weeks of Sickness," which he so pathetically describes in his *Reliquiæ Juveniles*, he had been carried by Sir Thomas Abney to his villa at Theobalds in Hertfordshire, and continued to reside in his family as his chaplain, and after the death of Sir Thomas continued in the same character with his widow. Here he composed many of those works for which his name will long be gratefully remembered by persons in various walks of life, and of various denominations in religion; and here he received that kind and respectful attention, which administers so much comfort to a weak and tender constitution, especially in the decline of life, and the decay of mental powers. He died here Nov. 25, 1748, aged 74, and was buried in the Dissenters burying ground in Bunhill Fields, but has lately had a monument erected to his memory in Westminster Abbey. Lady Abney died Jan. 12, 1749-50, and was buried in her family vault

---

* Sir Edward Abney, knt. member for the borough of Leicester, temp. Gul. & Mar. & Gul. III. is thought to have been his eldest son, and to have been the father of Sir Thomas Abney, knt. who was successively a baron of the Exchequer, and a judge of the court of Common Pleas, and died of the gaol distemper May 19, 1750, leaving issue a son, Thomas Abney, now of Willesley, esq. who has issue Parnel, sole daughter and heiress.

in the chancel, having had issue one son, who died between six and seven years of age, and three daughters, Sarah, who died unmarried in March 1732, and was buried with her father; Mary, married to Jocelyn Pickard, now of Bloxworth, in the county of Dorset, esq. (son of Thomas Pickard, esq. citizen of London, and his wife Sarah, fourth daughter of Sir Robert Jocelyn, bart.) who died without issue, and was also buried with her father (and after her decease Mr. Pickard married a lady of the Trenchard family, by whom he has two sons, Thomas, of Lincoln's Inn, and the Rev. George Pickard), and Elizabeth, who thus became sole daughter and heiress, and died here unmarried, aged 78, on August 20, 1782, and was buried with her mother. She bore quarterly Abney and Gunston. She died possessed of this manor, which she held by lease from the prebendary during the lives of herself, of Thomas Abney, of Willesley, esq. and of Thomas Streatfeild, of Stoke Newington, esq. which lease, together with the rest of her property in this parish, she directed by her will to be sold.

In this parish stands a good old house, said to have been built about the latter end of the reign of queen Elizabeth, which, with a good garden, and about eight acres of land, was the property of Charles Fleetwood, also of Armingland Hall, in the county of Norfolk, esq. He was lieutenant-general of the army during the protectorate of Oliver Cromwell; and married to his second wife Bridget, eldest daughter of Cromwell, and widow of lieutenant-general Henry Ireton *, lord deputy of Ireland, who died

at

---

* The issue of their marriage were Mrs. Bendysh and Mrs. Carter. The first of these ladies was that eccentric character, of whom, and the other descendants of the Cromwell family, so copious, curious, and entertaining an account is given by Mess. Say, Brooke, and Luson, in Mr. Hughes's Letters, vols. II. and III. She appears to have been an enthusiastic admirer, as well as, both in person and spirit, a perfect antitype, of that " chosen vessel, that first and greatest and best of man- " kind, her divinely inspired grandfather, who, next to the apostles, is the first " saint in Heaven, and is placed next to them." She resided at South Town, in Suffolk, a little mile from Yarmouth, from whence she used frequently to set out

for

at Limerick, Sept. 26, 1651, in which office he succeeded him Sept. 19, 1654, and in which he was himself succeeded by his brother-in-law Henry Cromwell, Nov. 24, 1657. It is said, that Cromwell had appointed Fleetwood his successor, by an instrument under his own hand, which however could never be found; and upon Cromwell's death, he, with colonel Desborough (who married one of Cromwell's sisters), became the head of the republican party of the army, which used to assemble at Wallingford House*. On April 6, 1659, the officers of the army petitioned Richard Cromwell, desiring Fleetwood for their general. On the 22d they obliged him to dissolve the new parliament, and in a few days after unanimously elected Fleetwood their general. On May 7, they restored the remains of the Long Parliament (which had been dissolved by Oliver, April 20, 1653), called in derision the Rump, who in a few days obliged Richard Cromwell to resign the protectorate, and appointed Fleetwood commander in chief of the land forces of the commonwealth of England, Scotland, and Ireland for one year. However, this commission was annulled by the parliament from Oct. 11 following; but on the 13th, the officers of the army by violence prevented the members from assembling, and thus produced a perfect anarchy of ten days. They then again declared Fleetwood their general, and on the 26th agreed to establish a committee of safety for the administration of the government, consisting of 23 persons, of whom he was one; but " at last" (says Rapin, Hist. of England, Book 22) " his collegues and himself wanting

for home at about one o'clock in the morning, alone, riding upon, or drawn by, an old favourite mare, and singing " a psalm, or one of Watts's hymns, in a very " loud, but not a very harmonious key." Her sister was the wife " of Mr. Carter, " a wealthy merchant of Yarmouth," in Norfolk. It appears by our register, that Mr. Nathaniel Carter, of *Yearmouth*, was married by licence to Mrs. Mary Fleetwood, Feb. 21, 1677 8. Can this be the same person? Was her name mistaken by the registrar, as she was the daughter of Mrs. Fleetwood? Or had she dropped the name of Ireton, because her father signed the warrant for the murder of the king?

* Q. Where was Wallingford House? Somewhere, it is believed, in or near the Strand.

" capacity

                                                                1st wife
                                                                Barbara,
                                                                and heir
                                                                drew Fr
                                                                of Londo

Joan Cheney.=Everard.   Rol
                         Fra
                         a m
             John.   156

Anne =Sir Miles, of   Ge
Luke. │ Aldwinkle,
        co. Nor-
        thampton,
        receiver of
        the court
        of wards.

George, who is   William
suppofed to have   Roger.
figned the warrant Charles.
for the murder of
king Charles; to
have been knight-
ed by Cromwell,
Sept. 15, 1655 or   Mary,
6; and to have been knt of l

Pedigree of FLEETWOOD.

John Fleetwood, of Plumpton Parva.=....

Henry, of Plumpton,=...
3 Hen. VI.

Edmund, living = Elizabeth, daughter
13 Edw. IV | of Robert Holland,
of Holland.

William of Hesketh,=Elena, da. of Ro-
co. Lancaster esq. | bert Standish.

Notes (right margin):
** Besides the names included herein, the f
burials of the parish of Stoke Newin.
"Mr Charles Fleetwood", the *Sone* of Mr
This was probably an infant son of Smith Fleet
"Mr Charles Fleetwood, the *Sone* of &c.
This is supposed to be a younger son of the
proof of this
" A still-born child of Mr Smith Fleetwoo
" Anne Fleetwood, the wife of Mr Smith
was probably mother of the preceding, and
wife, but there is no positive proof of this
" Ellen Fleetwood buried in a velvet coffin
to her, I have not the least means of informa

	2 2d wife		3		4
da.=Thomas, of the Vache,	=Bridget, da.	John of Penwortham,	Robert.=....		Edmund, monk
of An- co. Bucks, comp-	of Sir John	co. Lancaster, liv-			of Sion, co.
cis, troller of the mint,	Spring, knt.	ing 1569, ancestor to			Middlesex.
on. Southwark, and sur-	of Lavenham,	Sir Tho. Fleetwood,	William of Missenden-abbey, co. Bucks, born at
veyor of the king's	co. Suffolk,	bart. of Caldwich, co.	Oxon, and of the Middle Temple, elected recorder
possessions in Cheshire,	living 1570.	Stafford.	Term 1580, surrendered the recordership 1591, (a)
2 Edw. VI. ob. Nov			the celebrated chief justice of both benches) m
1, 1570, ag. 52.			the fellows of the original society of antiquaries.

bert.	Margaret.=Robert	Sir William,=Jane, da of Wil-	Henry=Elizabeth, d	Sir Geo. of	Edmund, an-
ncis,	Dormer,	of Crasford,	liam Clifton, sister	of Edw. Fust,	the Vache,	cestor of the
nor,	living	receiver of	of Gervase lord	of London.	from whom	Fleetwoods
9	1569.	the court of	Clifton, relict of		many de-	of Roshall,
		wards.	... Copleston.		scendants.	co. Lancaster

rard.=Elizabeth	Thomas.	1st wife	2d wife	George, went into=	....Gyl-
Lambert.	John.	=Sir William, knt. cup=	...Hervey.	Sweden, was a fa-	lenstierna, a
	Hester.	bearer to James I and		mous general, and	Swedish lady,
	Bridget.	Charles I comptroller		created a baron.	and left issue.
	Catherine.	of Woodstock-park.			
	Joan.				
	Elizabeth.				

Dorothy.	Sir Miles, of	Colonel	Other	2d wife	1st wife
Anne.	Aldwinkle, co.	William.	sons.	Bridget, eldest=CHARLES Fleetwood, of Armingland-hall, =Frances
Martha.	Northampton,			da. of Oliver	co. Norfolk, and of Stoke Newington,	Smith.
Elizabeth.	knt.			Cromwell, re-	co. Middlesex, esq. lord deputy of Ire-
				lict of Henry	land, temp. Usurp. and general of the
				Ireton, marr.	army before the Restoration, died at Stoke
				circa 1653, ob.	Newington soon after the Revolution.
				s. p. 1681	

da. of Sir John Coke, =Sir Edward Hartopp, bart. of Freathby, co. Leic. d. 1657, son of Sir

llowing appear in the register of

...th Fleetwood, 1 Oct 1675"
...od and Mary Hartopp
..., Fleetwood, 14 May 1676"
General, but there is no positive

...1 Jan 1682
...etwood, 29 Feb 1683 " This
...ppeared to have been a second

...Jun, 1701 " With regard

...Penworth, co. Lanc. of Brazen Nose College,
...r of London 1571, chosen serjeant at law Mich.
...d was succeeded by Edward Coke, esq. afterwards
...a queen's serjeant 27 Jan. 1592, and one of
...ob. Feb. 28, 1594, buried at Great Missenden.

Edward,
and other
children.

Symon Smith, of === ...
Beccles, co. Suff. esq. | Robert.

Thomas, of Winston, === ...
co. Norfolk, esq. | Champion.

Symon, of Winston, === Elizabeth, da.   Nicholas.
1664, and of Felt- | and heir of Sir
well in right of his | Edmund Mun-
wife. | diford, of Felt-
                   | well, c. Nor-
                   | folk, knight.

imprisoned in the Tower for life, after the Restoration.

Charles Fleetwood, of Armingland-hall and Winston, esq. ob cœlebs

Smith Fleet of Arminglan Winston, and Dalling, esq at Wood Dalli Oct. 1726, æ

Elizabeth, bur. at Dal

| Charles Hartopp, b. 5 June 1672 ob. infans. | Edward Hartopp, ob. inf. bur. at Stoke Newington, 25 January, 1675-6. | John Hartopp, ob inf. bur. at Stoke Newington, 28 May 1679 | Sarah, da of Joseph Woolfe, alderman of London, ob 12 Sept. 1730, æt. 35, bur. at Stoke Newington. | Sir John topp, of by, bap Jan. 176 bur at Newing |

Joseph Hurlock, esq late governor of Bencoolen, living 1783. =Sarah, ob. 27 March 1766, æt. 47, bur. at Stoke Newington.   Eli. Jos 178

Edmund Bunny, of Leicester, esq now Edmund Craddock Hartopp, of Newbold and Aston Flamville, co. Leic. and Mericale-priory, co. Warw 1783. =Ann, sole da born at S ok 1 April, 17

Two daughters.

† See Blomefield, Norf I 501
Blomefield fays, his brother Cha
‡ Where his father, formerly

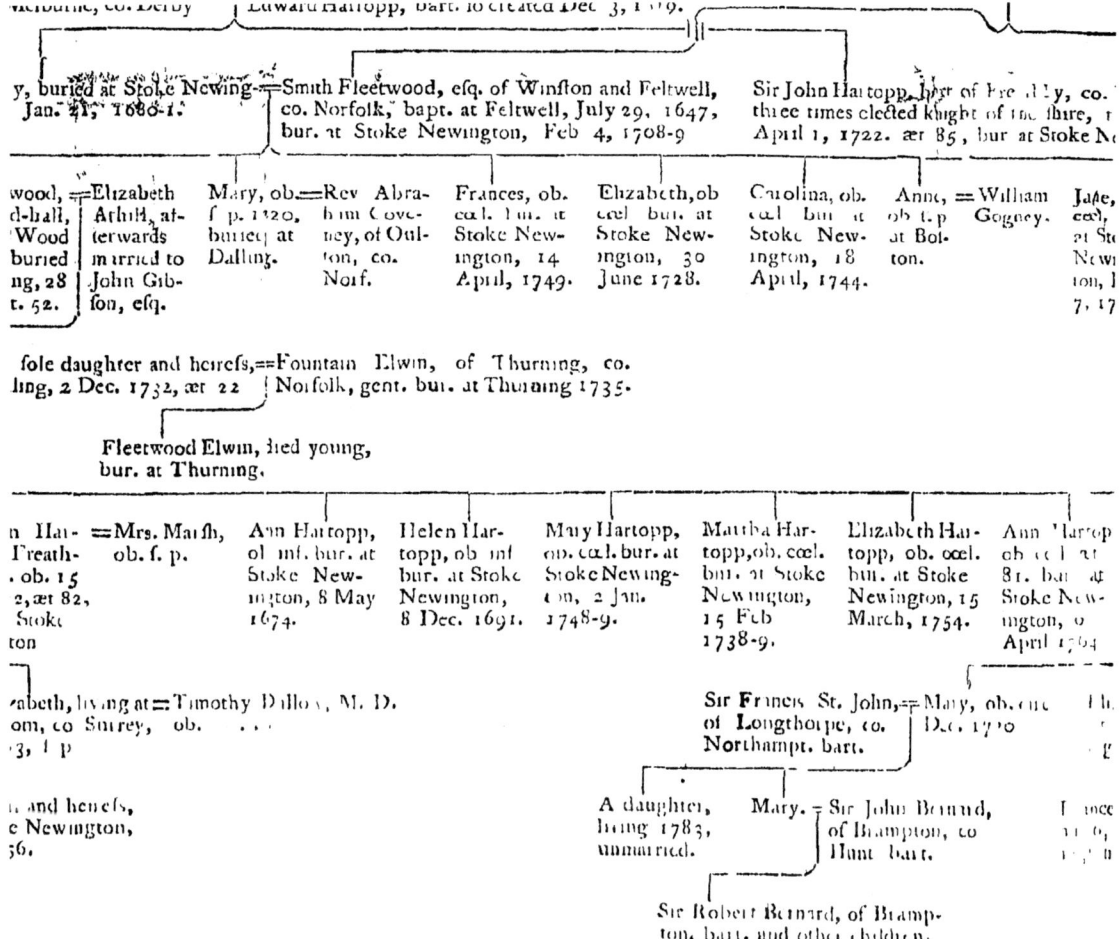

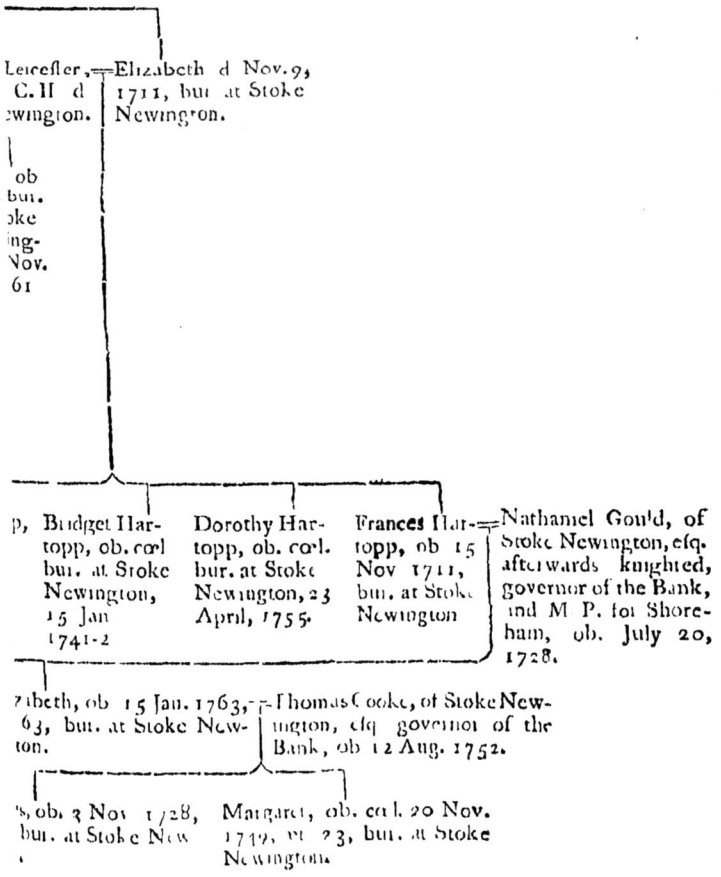

"capacity and resolution, consented to the meeting of parliament
"(Dec. 26), and voluntarily resigned their usurped authority.
"They had no sooner given their consent, than they were en-
"tirely abandoned by their whole party." To compleat this account of "the lord general," it will be proper to subjoin what is
said of him in Neal's Hist. of Puritans, vol. IV. cap. 4. that "when
"he found he could not keep the army within bounds, who
"were for new changes, he retired from public business, and
"spent the remainder of his life privately among his friends at
"Stoke Newington, where he died soon after the Revolution, be-
"ing more remarkable for piety and devotion, than for courage
"or deep penetration in politics." The precise time of his death,
and the place of his burial, I cannot ascertain. There is an en-
try in our register of the burial of "Bridget Fleetwood, in the
"church, on 5 Sept. 1681," who, I suppose, was his second
wife. General Fleetwood married to his first wife, Frances, sole
daughter and at length heiress of Thomas Smith, of Winston, in the county of Norfolk, esq. by whom he had issue a
daughter Elizabeth, and a son Smith, born at Feltwell St. Mary,
in the said county, 1647, who married Mary, daughter of Sir
Edward Hartopp, bart. They had issue two sons and six
daughters; Charles Fleetwood, of Armingland Hall and Winston, esq. who died unmarried, and was succeeded in his
estates by his brother, Smith Fleetwood, of Wood Dalling, esq.
at which place he was buried Oct. 28, 1726, aged 52. He
married Elizabeth, daughter of Mr. Athill (who was afterwards
married to John Gibson, esq.) by whom he had issue Elizabeth,
sole daughter and heiress, married to Fountain Elwin, of Thurning, gent. and buried at Dalling, Dec. 2, 1732, in the 22d
year of her age. She has an atchievement in this church, bearing Argent a Chevron engrailed Gules, between 3 martlets Sable, *Elwin*; impaled with party per pale nebulée Or and Azure,
6 martlets, 2, 2, and 2, counterchanged, *Fleetwood*. She had issue
only one child, Fleetwood Elwin, who died young, and was buried
at Thurning, as his father also was in 1735. Upon her death, the

estates

estates became the joint property of the survivors of the six sisters of her father the last Smith Fleetwood, who were, 1. Mary, married to the Rev. Abraham Coveney, of Oulton, in Norfolk, died without issue 1720, and is buried at Dalling. 2. Frances, died here unmarried, and was buried in the church April 14, 1749. 3. Elizabeth, died unmarried, and was buried here June 30, 1728. 4. Carolina, died here unmarried, and was buried April 18, 1744. 5. Anne, married to William Gogney, died at Bolton without issue. 6. Jane, died here unmarried, and was buried Nov. 7, 1761. This lady and her sister Frances, the two last descendants of the male line of the family, resided in a house that they rented of the lady of the manor, being parcel of the demesne *.

We now return to Elizabeth, sister to Smith Fleetwood, esq. who married the daughter of Sir Edward Hartopp, bart. which Elizabeth was the wife of his son and successor, Sir John Hartopp, of Freathby, in the county of Leicester, bart. for which county he was three times elected member, temp. Car. II. to whom this estate devolved. He bore Sable, a chevron Ermine between 3 otters passant Argent, with an inescutcheon of the arms of Ulster. Lady Hartopp died Nov. 9, 1711, and Sir John April 1, 1722, in the 85th year of his age, and were both buried in this church. They appear to have had issue four sons and nine daughters; Charles, born June 5, 1672, died young; Edward, buried in the family vault Jan. 25, 1675-6; John, buried with his brother, May 28, 1679; a second John, who succeeded his father, and married Sarah, daughter of Sir Joseph Woolfe, of Hackney, knt. alderman of London, who died Sept. 12, 1730, aged 35, and was buried here, leaving issue two daughters, of whom one was Sarah, married in June 1755 to Joseph Hurlock,

* It is with pleasure I embrace this opportunity of acknowledging how much this little work has been improved by the information received from Mr. Nichols, the printer of it, in several instances, and particularly by his communication of the extract from Domesday, the pedigree of Mr. Dudley, and this of the family of Fleetwood.

esq.

esq. late governor of Bencoolen, and afterwards a director of the East India Company, but died March 27, 1766, aged 47, and was also buried here, leaving issue one daughter Anne, who thus became heiress and representative of the families of Hartopp and Fleetwood, and, by the will of the abovementioned Mrs. Jane Fleetwood, came into possession of the estates of that family in the county of Norfolk. She was married August 8, 1777, to Edmund Bunny, esq. of Leicester, who was afterwards empowered by act of parliament to take and use the names of Cradock for his mother, and Hartopp for his wife's estates, and served the office of sheriff of the county of Leicester in 1781; they have two daughters. Elizabeth, the other daughter and co-heiress of the late Sir John Hartopp, was married circa Dec. 1759, to Timothy Dallow, M. D. whom she survives, but has no issue. Sir John Hartopp, many years after the death of his first lady, married Mrs. Marsh, and died without issue by her Jan. 15, 1762, aged 82, and was buried here, when the title became extinct, and his widow died not very long after him. Of the nine sisters of this Sir John Hartopp, eight died here unmarried, and were buried in the church on the days hereafter mentioned, *viz.* Anne, May 8, 1674*; Helen, Dec. 8, 1691; Mary, Jan. 2, 1748-9; Martha, Feb. 15, 1738-9 (I am not certain that she stands in her proper place according to her age); Elizabeth, March 15, 1754; a second Anne, April 6, 1764*, aged 81; Bridget, Jan. 15, 1741-2; Dorothy, April 23, 1755; the other, Frances, died Nov. 15, 1711, six days after her mother, and was also buried here, being then the wife of Nathaniel Gould, of this parish, esq. a Turkey merchant, and governor of the Bank of England in that and the following year, who was knighted after her death. This estate (which was enlarged by the purchase of more land) was now become his property, and he enlarged the house, or rather built a new one adjoining to it, where he resided, and in

* Surely very few families can be produced in which one sister has died at the distance of *ninety* years from another. *Rara avis in terris!*

which

which he died July 20, 1728, having had issue two daughters, of whom one was Mary, married to Sir Francis St. John, of Longthorpe, in the county of Northampton, bart. which lady died circa Dec. 1720, leaving issue two daughters, of whom one is unmarried now, and resides in Wimple Street, Cavendish Square, and near Welwyn, Hertfordshire; and the other, Mary, was married to the late Sir John Bernard, of Brampton, in the county of Huntington, bart. Elizabeth, the other daughter and co-heiress of Sir Nathaniel Gould, was married to Thomas Cooke, of this parish, esq. also a Turkey merchant, many years in the commission of the peace for this county, and governor of the Bank in the years 1737, 8, and 9, where his name probably is still remembered, for he made a present of 1000*l.* to the clerks. He had issue two daughters, who both died unmarried, and were buried in the church, Frances Nov. 3, 1728, aged six, and Margaret Nov. 20, 1749, aged 23. Mr. Cooke died here Aug. 12, 1752, and by his own direction was carried to Morden College, Blackheath, of which he was a trustee; there he was taken out of his coffin (which was laid by for the use of the first pensioner that might need it) and set upright in the earth close to a style very near the college. His widow died Jan. 15, 1763, aged 63, and was buried by her children. Sir Nathaniel Gould left the estate here to her for her life, and she lived and died in his house, the more ancient part of the edifice being the residence of her aunts, and of the family of Hurlock; after her decease it was to revert to the male heirs of her father, but she had procured a lease of the ancient part of the house for seven years, to commence from that time, for the use of her still surviving aunt, soon after whose death the whole was sold by John Gould, esq. nephew to Sir Nathaniel, to George Perrott, esq. one of the barons of the Exchequer, who resided for several years in Sir Nathaniel Gould's house, and at his death left the estate by will to his sister Mary, now the widow of the late Rev. John Territt, M. A. vicar of South Weald, in Essex.

On the West side of the London road, near the two mile stone, lies a piece of land, containing about six acres, supposed to be the land referred to in the bequest of John Stocker, esq. mentioned in p. 13, abutting West on a certain field lane, and East on the said road, whereon stands a little hamlet, now containing 10 houses, known by the name of *The Palatine Houses*, the origin of which, as well as of the name it bears, will appear from the following orders of vestry: "1709, Aug. 15. Agreed, That
" this parish is willing to settle four families of the Palatines, to
" the number not exceeding 20 persons, at the rate of 5*l.* per
" head, provided that other parishes do the same. Sept. 26.
" Resolved, That the churchwardens and Mr. (Thomas) Thomp-
" son do agree with some person to build four houses in the pa-
" rish field. Resolved, That Nathaniel Gould, esq. do choose
" two families of the Palatines to be inhabitants of two of the
" said houses."

A TABLE, exhibiting the rights of the parishioners of Stoke Newington, and the several donations and benefactions to the said parish, compiled in pursuance of an order of vestry made August 13, 1764, and now hanging in the vestry-room.

"The parishioners of Stoke Newington are seised in fee of a customary piece of land lying in the said parish, and containing about six acres, and formerly called and known by the name of *The Gravel Pit Field*, and upon which certain buildings, known by the name of *The Palatine Houses*, are now erected and standing.

Mr. WILLIAM STEPHENS, formerly of this parish, by his last will bearing date Sept. 11, 1638, and proved in the Prerogative court of the archbishop of Canterbury Jan. 22, 1639, gave the sum of 10*l.* for a stock for the poor of this parish, and the sum of 3*l.* more to be diftributed among the poor; he likewife devifed to the parfon and churchwardens for the time being, of this parifh, and to their fucceffors for ever, to the ufe of the poor of this parifh, an annuity or yearly rent-charge 5*l.* to be for ever iffuing out of his copyhold lands lying in the parifh of Hornfey, and to be paid on the feaft of the Nativity of our Lord God in every year. The faid Mr. Stephens likewife gave to this parifh a large filver flagon and chalice, with a cover.

THOMAS STOCK, efq. formerly of this parifh, by his laft will bearing date May 3, 1664, and proved in the Prerogative court of the archbifhop of Canterbury the 26th of the fame month, gave and devifed the rent of the firft houfe, next adjoining to Robert Roberts's, now known by the fign of the Three Crowns, and the houfe next adjoining to that, to the poor of this parifh; and he gave the rent of the third houfe towards teaching and educating five poor people's children of this parifh in the fear of God; and the rent of the fifth houfe he gave towards bringing the New River water down the Street, if that bufinefs fhould take effect within three years; and if the work fhould not take effect within that time, then he directed that the rent of it fhould go towards keeping in repair the other three, and that the furplus fhould be given to the poor; and he left the truft of feeing the rents of thefe four houfes difpofed according to his will, to his wife and his fon Edge for their lives, and afterwards to the church-wardens of this parifh for the time being, and four of the ancients of the parifh, to be chofen occafionally by the veftry.

SIDRACH SIMPSON, D. D. formerly rector of this parifh, by his laft will dated Oct. 11, 1704, and proved in the Prerogative court of the archbifhop of Canterbury, Nov. 4, following, charged a copyhold brick meffuage, and three acres of land, lying within the manor of Stoke Newington (and which he thereby gave and devifed to the ufe of the incumbent rector or minifter of the church of Stoke Newington aforefaid, for the time being,

and

and to his succeffors for ever, incumbent of the said church, during such time as each of them should continue incumbent and officiate in the cure of Stoke Newington aforesaid), with the payment of the sum of 50s. *per annum* for ever, to be given to the poor of this parish in bread on Sunday in every week, in equal portions, and as the rector for the time being should appoint.

ELIZABETH BAKER, widow, formerly of this parish, by her last will dated Aug. 18, 1716, and proved in the Prerogative Court of the archbishop of Canterbury the 21st of the same month, bequeathed to the churchwardens of this parish for the time being, and to their succeffors, the sum of 50l. upon trust, to place the same sum at interest upon parliamentary or real securities, and to lay out an equal proportion of such interest in bread to be by them distributed in two-penny loaves on Sunday in every week, amongst six poor widows; and in case six in number should not appear to receive the same, then the whole quantity of bread is directed to be distributed to so many of them under that number as should appear to receive it; or to one only, if no more should appear.

On April 8, 1711, the Rev. Dr. JOHN MILLINGTON, the rector of this parish, gave to the use of the parish a piece of plate or dish, to be used at the offertory. And on April 15, 1723, the same gentleman gave a clock for the parish church.

GEORGE GREEN, esq. late of this parish, by his last will dated Aug. 12, 1762, and proved in the Prerogative Court of the archbishop of Canterbury March 26, 1764, gave and bequeathed to the minister and churchwardens of this parish for the time being, and to their succeffors for ever, the sum of 20s. a year, issuing out of his copyhold estate in this parish, to be laid out in bread, and distributed to the poor of this parish upon the 12th day of December in every year. He likewise bequeathed to the said minister and churchwardens the sum of 100*l.* to be placed out at interest on government or other good securities; and he gave the sum of 50*s.* a year, part of the interest and produce thereof, towards the support of the charity-school in this parish, as long as the same should subsist; and in case the said charity-school should not be carried on, then he directed that the said 50*s.* a year should be applied in placing out every other year (so that the sum should always amount to 5*l.*) some poor child born in this parish apprentice to some honest trade, at the nomination and appointment of the said minister and church wardens for ever; and he directed that the remaining part of the interest of the said 100*l.* should be distributed by the minister and church-wardens of this parish for the time being, amongst the poor inhabitants of this parish, upon the 12th day of December in every year, in such proportions as their necessities should require; and he directed that the account of the interest of the said 100*l.* should be entered yearly in the vestry-book in the church-wardens accounts.

On August 13, 1764, the Rev. WILLIAM HENRY NICOLLS, the rector of this parish, gave two communion-books, printed in folio on royal paper, to be used at the communion."

Thus far the table; but this table is very imperfect, for, as already appears from this work, the names of WILLIAM PATTEN*, esq. THOMAS SUTTON†, esq. and capt. EDWARD ALANSON‡, are very unjustly omitted; to which should be added the following:

SIDRACH SIMPSON, D. D. in addition to the bequests mentioned in pages 34 and 35, by his last will gave and devised to the use of the rector of this parish for the time being, a certain copyhold messuage or tenement, with a little land thereto adjoining, held of the manor of Hackney, which messuage stands on the East side of the London road, very near the new buildings South of Kingsland turnpike.

* See p. 20. † See p. 24. ‡ See p. 12.

John Stevens, citizen and stationer of London, who died Feb. 3, 1726-7, left by will 10l. to be put out at interest, and the produce to be laid out in bread, to be given to the poor at Christmas in every year.

John Millington, D. D. also by his last will left to the dean and chapter of St. Paul's, certain copyhold lands, containing 24 acres and a half, held of the manor of Acton, in the county of Middlesex, two thirds of the produce of which is to be paid by the said dean and chapter to the rector of this parish for the time being; he also left 5l. to the poor of the parish.

Thomas Thompson, late of this parish, gent. by his will dated June 11, 1729, gave two guineas per annum towards maintaining the charity-school in Stoke Newington, to be paid out of the Palatine-houses during the continuance of the lease (which expires at Michaelmas 1809), if the school should be kept up so long; and he gave to the poor of Newington 5l.

John Newman, late of Newington Green, in this Parish, gent. who died Oct. 24, 1729, by his will devised to his trustees, Dr. Nicholas Robinson, Richard Hoare, esq. and Mr. Southouse *(inter alia)* two or three messuages or tenements, situated near Wapping New Stairs, in trust for the founding, supporting, and maintaining such charity-schools as they thought proper to bestow the same upon; and they have for a series of years given the yearly sum of 6l. towards the support of this charity-school.

Mrs. Sarah Beardsley, of this parish, widow, in February 1745, gave the great Bible used in the reading desk.

Miss Mary Hammond, late of this parish, who died Feb. 12, 1774, by her will dated Dec. 22, 1772, gave and bequeathed to the rector and churchwardens for the time being, 100l. upon trust, to invest the same in their names in the purchase of some of the public stocks or funds, and to pay and apply the yearly dividends and interest thereof towards supporting and maintaining the charity-school established in the said parish, so long as the same shall subsist and be carried on; but when such school shall

shall ceafe and be difcontinued, then to pay and apply every fecond year the accumulated dividends and intereft for the putting out, with the confent and approbation of the inhabitants affembled in veftry, fome poor child born in the faid parifh as an apprentice, to learn fome ufeful trade and employment.

Mrs. ELIZABETH ABNEY, lady of this manor, by her laft will dated June 10, 1782, and proved in the Prerogative Court of the archbifhop of Canterbury on Aug. 23 following, bequeathed 100*l.* to the poor of the parifh and town of Stoke Newington.

Befides the benefactions above fpecified, John Duddeleye, efq. left a legacy to the poor of the parifh, and another towards the mending of Iflington Lane, as it is called in his will*. THOMAS GUNSTON, efq. left 30*l.* Mrs. DEE, in 1728, 5*l.*: and Mrs. JANE FLEETWOOD, in 1761, a legacy, to the poor of the parifh. Other perfons have probably left legacies to the poor; but they being immediately diftributed, and no eftablifhment formed in confequence, it would be difficult to find any record of them, but in the wills of the refpective teftators, or poffibly in the parifh books.

---

* It is with pleafure I embrace this opportunity of bearing teftimony to the honour of the Prerogative Office, by informing the curious enquirer that the copies of the wills in the earlier ages of the office are perfectly fair, neat, and legible. I fpeak from ocular demonftration as to the book which contains the will of Mr. Duddeleye, and do not doubt, from the fairnefs and accuracy of the indexes, but the fame may be inferred with refpect to thofe of a ftill earlier date; they begin with the year 1383, in the primacy of the moft rev. father in God William Courtney, lord archbifhop of Canterbury; but the number for the two firft centuries is fo exceedingly fmall, that all that time may be juftly deemed the infancy of the office.

APPENDIX,

APPENDIX, N° I. (see p. 12.)

Dr. SAMUEL WRIGHT was born January 30, 1682-3, being eldest son of Mr. James Wright, a Nonconformist minister at Retford, in the county of Nottingham, by Mrs. Eleanor Cotton, daughter of Mr. Cotton, a gentleman of Yorkshire, and sister to the Rev. Mr. Thomas Cotton of Westminster, whose funeral sermon his Nephew preached and published. At eleven years old he lost his father, being then at school at Attercliffe in Yorkshire, whence he removed to Darton in the same county, about six miles from Wakefield, under the care of his grandmother and his uncle Cotton. At sixteen he studied under the care of the Rev. Mr. Jollie, who kept an academy at Attercliffe, whom about the age of twenty-one he quitted, and went to his uncle's house at the Haigh, where he officiated as his chaplain; and after his death he came to London, having preached only three or four sermons in the country. He lived a little while in his uncle's family at St. Giles's, and thence went to be chaplain to lady Susannah Lort at Turnham-green, and was chosen to preach the Lord's-day evening lecture at Mr. Cotton's at St. Giles's. Being soon after invited to assist Dr. Grosvenor at Crosby-square meeting, he quitted lady Lort and St. Giles's, and was soon after chosen to carry on an evening lecture in Southwark, in conjunction with the Rev. Mr. Haman Hood; who soon quitting it, it devolved on Mr. Wright, then only twenty-three.

On the death of Mr. Matthew Sylvester, 1708, he was chosen pastor of the congregation at Blackfriars, which increased considerably under his care, and where he continued many years, till he removed to Carter-lane, which meeting-house was built for him, and opened by him Dec. 5, 1734, with a Sermon on 2 Chron. vi. 40. His sermons printed singly amount to near forty: among them funeral ones for Mr. Caleb Head, 1707; Dr. Upton, 1711; Rev. Joseph Coningham, 1716; Mr. John Mills, merchant, 1717; the Rev. Thomas Cotton, 1730; Mrs. Elizabeth Hughes, 1735; Rev. Mr. John Munckley, father of the late Dr. Nicholas Munckley, 1738. Among those against Popery at the Salters Hall Lecture is one by him preached February 6, 1734-5, intituled, "Scripture and Tradition considered," from Ephes. ii. 20. He preached another at the Old Jewry before the Society for the relief of Dissenting Ministers widows and children, 1738. Among the sermons preached by him at Blackfriars, was one " on the Marriage of the Prince of " Orange," March 17, 1734, being the Sunday after the event. A sermon or tract on " The Obligation of Virtue," which he founded solely on the will of God. An Answer to it, in defence of Dr. Clarke's Scheme, was written by the Rev. Thomas Mole, then minister at Rotherhithe. " The great concern of Human " Life," first printed without his name 1729, and " Three discourses on Self-" possession." " Justice in all its branches," 1720. " Charity in all its branches," 1730. " A Treatise on the Deceitfulness of Sin." " Knowledge and Charity " considered separately and united. A Sermon preached at Nottingham, July 16, " 1732." But his most considerable work was his Treatise on the New Birth, or,

" That

"That being born again, without which it is impoffible to enter into the kingdom of God," which had gone through fifteen editions before his death.

Dr. Wright is traditionally underftood to have been the author of the fong, "Happy Hours, all Hours excelling." He was remarkable for the melody of his voice, and the beauty of his elocution. Archbifhop Herring, when a young man, frequently attended him as a model of delivery, not openly in the Meeting-houfe, but in a large porch belonging to the old place in Blackfriars.

He married in 1710 the widow of his predeceffor Mr. Sylvefter, daughter of the Rev. Mr. Obadiah Hughes, minifter of the diffenting congregation at Enfield, aunt to the late Dr. Obadiah Hughes, by whom he had one fon, fince dead, a tradefman in the city, and one daughter, married to a citizen in Newgate Street, a moft accomplifhed woman, but who became the victim of her own imprudence.

He died April 3, 1746, at Newington Green, which was his refidence. His funeral fermon was preached at Carter Lane meeting by Dr. Milner; another at the fame place by Dr. Obadiah Hughes, who wrote his epitaph. He was fucceeded by Mr. Thomas Newman, who had been many years his affiftant, and was on his death, 1758, fucceeded by Mr. Edward Pickard, with whom was firft affociated Mr. John Tailer, from Stow-Market, in Suffolk, and after his death, Mr. Thomas Tayler, chaplain to Mrs. Abney, and who was fome years affiftant tutor to the Diffenting Academy at Daventry. Upon Mr. Pickard's deceafe, Feb. 10, 1778, aged 64, Mr. Tayler fucceeded him in the paftoral charge of the fociety at Carter Lane, with whom is now affociated the Rev. Mr. John Fuller, late paftor of the Prefbyterian congregation at Enfield.

APPENDIX, N° II. (fee p. 25.)

A FUNERAL POEM, by Dr. WATTS, to the Memory of his honoured Friend THOMAS GUNSTON, efq. who died Nov. 11, 1700, when he had juft finifhed his Houfe at STOKE NEWINGTON.

Prefented to the Lady ABNEY, Lady Mayorefs of London, in July 1701.

OF blafted hopes, and of fhort withering joys,
Sing, heavenly Mufe. Try thine ethereal voice
In funeral numbers and a doleful fong;
Gunfton the juft, the generous, and the young,
Gunfton the friend is dead. O empty name
Of earthly blifs! 'tis all an airy dream,
All a vain thought! Our foaring fancies rife
On treacherous wings! and hopes that touch the fkies
Drag but a longer ruin through the downward air,
And plunge the falling joy ftill deeper in defpair.

How did our souls stand flatter'd and prepar'd
To shout him welcome to the seat he rear'd!
There the dear man should see his hopes complete,
Smiling, and tasting every lawful sweet
That peace and plenty brings, while numerous years
Circling delightful play'd around the spheres:
Revolving suns should still renew his strength,
And draw th' uncommon thread to an unusual length.
But hasty Fate thrusts her dread shears between,
Cuts the young life off, and shuts up the scene.
Thus airy pleasure dances in our eyes,
And spreads false images in fair disguise,
T' allure our souls, till just within our arms
The vision dies, and all the painted charms
Flee quick away from the pursuing sight,
Till they are lost in shades, and mingle with the night.

Muse, stretch thy wings, and thy sad journey bend
To the fair Fabrick that thy dying friend
Built nameless: 'twill suggest a thousand things
Mournful and soft as my Urania sings.

How did he lay the deep Foundations strong,
Marking the bounds, and rear the Walls along
Solid and lasting; there a numerous train
Of happy Gunstons might in pleasure reign,
While nations perish, and long ages run,
Nations unborn, and ages unbegun:
Not Time itself should waste the blest estate,
Nor the tenth race rebuild the ancient seat.
How fond our fancies are! The founder dies
Childless [*]: his sisters weep and close his eyes,
And wait upon his hearse with never-ceasing cries.
Lofty and slow it moves to meet the tomb,
While weighty sorrow nods on every plume;
A thousand groans his dear remains convey,
To his cold lodging in a bed of clay,
His country's sacred tears well-watering all the way.
See the dull wheels roll on the sable road;
But no dear son to tend the mournful load,
And fondly kind drop his young sorrows there,
The father's urn bedewing with a filial tear.
O had he left us One behind to play
Wanton about the painted Hall, and say,
" This was my father's!" with impatient joy
In my fond arms I'd clasp the smiling boy,

[*] There is a tradition, but I know not how well founded, that he intended to have married Mary, eldest (surviving) daughter of Sir John Hartopp, bart.

And call him my young friend: but awful Fate
Design'd the mighty stroke as lasting as 'twas great.
　And must this building then, this costly frame,
Stand here for strangers? Must some unknown name,
Possess these rooms, the labours of my friend?
Why were these walls rais'd for this hapless end?
Why these apartments all adorn'd so gay?
Why his rich fancy lavish'd thus away?
Muse, view the Paintings, how the hovering light
Plays o'er the colours in a wanton flight,
And mingled shades, wrought in by soft degrees,
Give a sweet foil to all the charming piece:
But night, eternal night, hangs black around
The dismal chambers of the hollow ground,
And solid shades unmingled round his bed
S and hideous Earthy fogs embrace his head,
And noisome vapours glide along his face,
Rising perpetual Muse, forsake the place,
Flee the raw damps of the unwholsome clay,
Look to his airy spacious Hall, and say,
" How has he chang'd it for a lonesome cave,
" Confin'd and crowded in a narrow grave!"
　Th' unhappy house looks desolate and mourns,
And every door groans doleful as it turns;
The pillars languish; and each lofty wall,
Stately in grief, laments the master's fall
In drops of briny dew, the fabrick bears
His faint resemblance, and renews my tears.
Solid and square it rises from below:
A noble air, without a gaudy show,
Reigns through the model, and adorns the whole;
Manly and plain. Such was the builder's soul.
　O how I love to view the stately frame,
That dear memorial of the best-lov'd name!
Then could I wish for some prodigious cave,
Vast as his fear, and silent as his grave,
Where the tall shades stretch to the hideous roof,
Forbid the day, and guard the sun-beams off;
Thither, my willing feet, should ye be drawn
At the grey twilight, and the early dawn.
There sweetly sad should my soft minutes roll,
Numbering the sorrows of my drooping soul.
But these are airy thoughts! substantial grief
Grows by those objects that should yield relief;
Fond of my woes, I heave my eyes around,
My grief from every prospect courts a wound;

Views the green gardens, views the smiling skies,
Still my heart sinks, and still my cares arise;
My wandering feet round the fair mansion rove,
And there, to sooth my sorrows, I indulge my love.
 Oft have I laid the awful Calvin by,
And the sweet Cowley, with impatient eye
To see those walls, pay the sad visit there,
And drop the tribute of an hourly tear:
Still I behold some melancholy scene,
With many a pensive thought, and many a sigh between.
Two days ago we took the evening air,
I, and my grief, and my Urania there;
Say, my Urania, how the western sun
Broke from black clouds, and in full glory shone
Gilding the roof, then dropt into the sea,
And sudden night devour'd the sweet remains of day;
Thus the bright youth just rear'd his shining head
From obscure shades of life, and sunk among the dead.
The rising sun, adorn'd with all his light,
Smiles on these walls again: but endless night
Reigns uncontrol'd where the dear Gunston lies,
He's set for ever, and must never rise.
Then why these beams, unseasonable star,
These lightsome smiles descending from afar,
To greet a mourning house? In vain the day
Breaks through the windows with a joyful ray,
And marks a shining path along the floors,
Bounding the evening and the morning hours;
In vain it bounds them: while vast emptiness }
And hollow silence reigns through all the place, }
Nor heeds the chearful change of Nature's face. }
Yet Nature's wheels will on without controul, }
The sun will rise, the tuneful spheres will roll, }
And the two nightly Bears walk round and watch the pole. }
 See while I speak, high on her sable wheel
Old Night advancing climbs the eastern hill:
Troops of dark clouds prepare her way; behold,
How their brown pinions edg'd with evening gold
Spread shadowing o'er the house, and glide away
Slowly pursuing the declining day;
O'er the broad Roof they fly their circuit still,
Thus days before they did, and days to come they will;
But the black cloud that shadows o'er his eyes
Hangs there unmoveable, and never flies:
Fain would I bid the envious gloom be gone; }
Ah fruitless wish! how are his curtains drawn }
For a long evening that despairs the dawn! }

Muse,

Muse, view the Turret: just beneath the skies
Lonesome it stands, and fixes my sad eyes,
As it would ask a tear. O sacred seat,
Sacred to friendship! O divine retreat!
Here did I hope my happy hours t' employ,
And fed before-hand on a promis'd joy,
When, weary of the noisy town, my friend
From mortal cares retiring, should ascend
And lead me thither. We alone would sit
Free and secure of all intruding feet:
Our thoughts should stretch their longest wings, and rise,
Nor bound their soarings by the lower skies:
Our tongues should aim at everlasting themes,
And speak what mortals dare, of all the names
Of boundless joys and glories, thrones and seats
Built high in heaven for souls: We'd trace the streets
Of Golden pavement, walk each blissful field,
And climb and taste the fruits the spicy mountains yield:
Then would we swear to keep the sacred road,
And walk right upwards to that blest abode:
We'd charge our parting spirits there to meet,
There hand in hand approach th' Almighty seat,
And bend our heads adoring at our Maker's feet.
Thus should we mount on bold adventurous wings
In high discourse, and dwell on heavenly things,
While the pleas'd hours in sweet succession move,
And minutes measur'd, as they are above,
By ever-circling joys, and ever-shining love.

 Anon our thoughts should lower their lofty flight,
Sink by degrees, and take a pleasing sight,
A large round prospect of the spreading plain,
The wealthy river, and his winding train,
The smoky city, and the busy men.
How we should smile, to see degenerate worms
Lavish their lives, and fight for airy forms
Of painted honour, dreams of empty sound,
Till envy rise, and shoot a secret wound
At swelling glory, strait the bubble breaks,
And the scenes vanish, as the man awakes;
Then the tall titles insolent and proud
Sink to the dust, and mingle with the crowd.

 Man is a restless thing. Still vain and wild,
Lives beyond sixty, nor outgrows the child:
His hurrying lusts still break the sacred bound
To seek new pleasures on forbidden ground,
And buy them all too dear. Unthinking fool,
For a short dying joy to sell a deathless soul!

'Tis but a grain of sweetness they can sow,
And reap the long sad harvest of immortal woe.
　Another tribe toil in a different strife,
And banish all the lawful sweets of life,
To sweat and dig for gold, to hoard the ore,
Hide the dear dust yet darker than before,
And never dare to use a grain of all the store.
　Happy the man that knows the value just
Of earthly things, nor is enslav'd to dust.
'Tis a rich gift the skies but rarely send
To favourite souls. Then happy thou, my friend,
For thou hadst learnt to manage and command
The wealth that heaven bestow'd with liberal hand:
Hence this fair structure rose; and hence this seat
Made to invite my not unwilling feet:
In vain 'twas made! for we shall never meet,
And smile, and love, and bless each other here;
The envious tomb forbids thy face t' appear,
Detains thee, Gunston, from my longing eyes,
And all my hopes lie bury'd, where my Gunston lies.
　Come hither, all ye tenderest souls, that know
The heights of fondness, and the depths of woe;
Young mothers, who your darling babes have found
Untimely murder'd with a ghastly wound;
Ye frighted nymphs, who on the bridal bed
Clasp'd in your arms your lovers cold and dead,
Come; in the pomp of all your wild despair,
With flowing eye-lids, and disorder'd hair,
Death in your looks; come, mingle grief with me,
And drown your little streams in my unbounded sea.
　You sacred mourners of a nobler mold,
Born for a friend, whose dear embraces hold
Beyond all nature's ties; you that have known
Two happy souls made intimately One,
And felt a parting stroke: 'Tis you must tell
The smart, the twinges, and the racks I feel:
This soul of mine that dreadful wound has borne,
Off from its side its dearest half is torn,
The rest lies bleeding, and but lives to mourn.
Oh infinite distress! such raging grief
Should command pity, and despair relief.
Passion, methinks, should rise from all my groans,
Give sense to rocks, and sympathy to stones.
　Ye dusky Woods and echoing Hills around,
Repeat my cries with a perpetual sound:
Be all ye flowery Vales with thorns o'ergrown,
Assist my sorrows, and declare your own;

Alas!

Alas! your lord is dead. The humble plain
Must ne'er receive his courteous feet again:
Mourn, ye gay smiling meadows, and be seen
In wintery robes, instead of youthful green;
And bid the Brook, that still runs warbling by,
Move silent on, and weep his useless channel dry.
Hither methinks the lowing herd should come,
And moaning turtles murmur o'er his tomb:
The oak shall wither, and the curling vine
Weep his young life out, while his arms untwine
Their amorous folds, and mix his bleeding soul with mine.
Ye stately elms, in your long order mourn*,
Strip off your pride, to dress your master's urn:
Here gently drop your leaves instead of tears:
Ye elms, the reverend growth of ancient years,
Stand tall and naked to the blustering rage
Of the mad winds, thus it becomes your age
To shew your sorrows. Often ye have seen
Our heads reclin'd upon the rising green;
Beneath your sacred shade diffus'd we lay,
Here friendship reign'd with an unbounded sway:
Hither our souls their constant offerings brought,
The burthens of the breast, and labours of the thought;
Our opening bosoms on the conscious ground
Spread all the sorrows and the joys we found,
And mingled every care; nor was it known
Which of the pains and pleasures were our own;
Then with an equal hand and honest soul
We share the heap, yet both possess the whole,
And all the passions there through both our bosoms roll.
By turns we comfort, and by turns complain,
And bear and ease by turns the sympathy of pain.

    Friendship! mysterious thing, what magic powers
Support thy sway, and charm these minds of ours!
Bound to thy foot we boast our birth right still,
And dream of freedom, when we've lost our will,
And chang'd away our souls: At thy command,
We snatch new miseries from a foreign hand,
To call them ours; and, thoughtless of our ease,
Plague the dear self that we were born to please.
Thou tyranness of minds, whose cruel throne
Heaps on poor mortals sorrows not their own;

---

* There was a long row of tall elms then standing where some years after the lower garden was made.

As though our mother Nature could no more
Find woes sufficient for each son she bore,
Friendship divides the shares, and lengthens out the store.
Yet we are fond of thine imperious reign,
Proud of thy slavery, wanton in our pain,
And chide the courteous hand when death dissolves the chain.
   Virtue, forgive the thought! The raving Muse
Wild and despairing knows not what she does,
Grows mad in grief, and in her savage hours
Affronts the name she loves and she adores.
She is thy votaress too; and at thy shrine,
O sacred Friendship, offer'd songs divine,
While Gunston liv'd, and both our souls were thine.
Here to these shades at solemn hours we came,
To pay devotion with a mutual flame,
Partners in bliss. Sweet luxury of the mind!
And sweet the aids of sense! Each ruder wind
Slept in its caverns, while an evening breeze
Fann'd the leaves gently, sporting through the trees:
The linnet and the lark their vespers sung,
And clouds of crimson o'er th' horizon hung;
The slow-declining sun with sloping wheels
Sunk down the golden day behind the western hills.
   Mourn, ye young gardens, ye unfinish'd gates,
Ye green inclosures, and ye growing sweets,
Lament; for ye our midnight hours have known,
And watch'd us walking by the silent moon
In conference divine, while heavenly fire
Kindling our breasts did all our thoughts inspire
With joys almost immortal; then our zeal
Blaz'd and burnt high to reach th' ethereal hill;
And love refin'd, like that above the poles,
Threw both our arms round one another's souls
In rapture and embraces. Oh forbear,
Forbear, my song! this is too much to bear,
Too dreadful to repeat; such joys as these
Fled from the earth for ever!—
   Oh for a general grief! let all things share
Our woes, that knew our loves: The neighbouring air
Let it be laden with immortal sighs,
And tell the gales, that every breath that flies
Over these fields should murmur and complain,
And kiss the fading grass, and propagate the pain;
Weep all ye buildings, and the groves around
For ever weep: this is an endless wound,

Vast and incurable. Ye buildings knew
His silver tongue, ye groves have heard it too:
At that dear sound no more shall ye rejoice,
And I no more must hear the charming voice:
Woe to my drooping soul! that heavenly breath,
That could speak life, lies now congeal'd in death;
While on his folded lips all cold and pale
Eternal chains and heavy silence dwell.

Yet my fond hope would hear him speak again,
Once more at least, one gentle word, and then
Gunston aloud I call. In vain I cry
Gunston aloud; for he must ne'er reply.
In vain I mourn, and drop these funeral tears,
Death and the Grave have neither eyes nor ears:
Wandering I tune my sorrows to the groves,
And vent my swelling griefs, and tell the winds our loves;
While the dear youth sleeps fast, and hears them not:
He hath forgot me: In the lonesome vault,
Mindless of Watts and Friendship, cold he lies,
Deaf and unthinking clay —

But whither am I led? This artless grief
Hurries the Muse on, obstinate and deaf
To all the nicer rules, and bears her down
From the tall fabrick to the neighbouring ground:
The pleasing hours, the happy moments past
In these sweet fields reviving on my taste
Snatch me away resistless with impetuous haste.

Spread thy strong pinions once again, my song,
And reach the Turret thou hast left so long:
O'er the wide roof its lofty head it rears,
Long waiting our converse; but only hears
The noisy tumults of the realms on high;
The winds salute it whistling as they fly,
Or jarring round the windows; rattling showers
Lash the fair sides; above, loud thunder roars;
But still the master sleeps; nor hears the voice
Of sacred friendship, nor the tempest's noise:
An iron slumber sits on every sense,
In vain the heavenly thunders strive to rouze it thence.

One labour more, my Muse, the golden sphere
Seems to demand. See through the dusky air
Downwards it shines upon the rising moon;
And, as she labours up to reach her noon,
Pursues her orb with repercussive light,
And streaming gold repays the paler beams of night:
But not one ray can reach the darksome grave,
Or pierce the solid gloom that fills the cave

Where Gunston dwells in death. Behold it flames
Like some new meteor with diffusive beams
Through the mid-heaven, and overcomes the stars;
" So shines thy Gunston's soul above the spheres,"
Raphael replies, and wipes away my tears.
" We saw the flesh sink down with closing eyes,
" We heard thy grief shriek out, He dies, He dies!
" Mistaken grief! to call the flesh the friend!
" On our fair wings did the bright youth ascend,
" All heaven embrac'd him with immortal love,
" And sung his welcome to the courts above.
" Gentle Ithuriel led him round the skies,
" The buildings struck him with immense surprize;
" The spires all radiant, and the mansions bright,
" The roof high-vaulted with ethereal light:
" Beauty and strength on the tall bulwarks sate
" In heavenly diamond; and for every gate
" On golden hinges a broad ruby turns,
" Guards off the foe, and as it moves it burns:
" Millions of glories reign through every part;
" Infinite power, and uncreated art,
" Stand here display'd, and to the stranger show
" How it out-shines the noblest seats below.
" The stranger fed his gazing powers awhile
" Transported: Then, with a regardless smile,
" Glanc'd his eye downward through the crystal floor,
" And took eternal leave of what he built before."
Now, fair Urania, leave the doleful strain;
Raphael commands: Assume thy joys again.
In everlasting numbers sing, and say,
" Gunston has mov'd his dwelling to the realms of day;
" Gunston the friend lives still: And give thy groans away."

APPENDIX, N° III. (see p. 18.)

Communicated by the Rev. ANDREW KIPPIS*, D.D. F.R.S. and S.A.

The Meeting-house at Newington Green was built in 1708.
    The first Minister of whom I can get an account was Mr RICHARD BISCOE, who left the place Dec. 25, 1727. Mr. Biscoe conformed, and became Chaplain in ordinary to King George II. Rector of St. Martin Outwich, London, and Prebendary of St. Paul's. He preached the Sermons at Boyle's Lecture, and formed

* To this gentleman I am also indebted for the greatest part of the account of Dr Wright

them into two volumes 8vo, 1742, in a work called "The History of the Acts of the Apostles." In this work he very much adopted the sentiments maintained by Lord Barrington, in his "Miscellanea Sacra."

When Mr. Biscoe quitted Newington Green, the Meeting-house was kept open by occasional supplies till Lady day 1729, when Mr. PATERSON was chosen Minister. He continued to preach there till Midsummer 1732, after which he conformed.

Mr. WHITEHEAR became Pastor of the congregation in the same year, and resided among them till 1736, when he was succeeded by Mr. LOVEDER, Librarian to Dr. Daniel Williams's Library. In 1738, Mr. Loveder, having resigned first the Library, and then his place at Newington Green, conformed to the Church of England, and obtained a living in Essex. He afterwards published in 8vo. a volume of Sermons, containing eight discourses.

The next Minister was HUGH WORTHINGTON, M. A. who was also Librarian. He removed to Leicester in 1742, where he is still living, the Pastor of a very respectable congregation. He is father of Mr. Hugh Worthington, jun. of Salters Hall, London, and has published two Charges, besides several occasional Sermons.

Mr. LEWIS, Librarian of Dr Williams's Library, succeeded Mr. Worthington; and afterwards removed to Maidstone, in Kent, where he died.

Mr. JOHN HOYLE, Librarian, was Mr. Lewis's successor. After some time he was chosen to be joint pastor at Norwich with Mr. Samuel Brown, in the room of Dr. John Taylor, and died at Norwich a few years after.

He was succeeded at Newington Green by Mr. RICHARD PRICE, now D. D. F. R. S. In 1770, Dr. Price became Pastor and Morning Preacher at the New Meeting House, Hackney; but still continues to preach at Newington Green in the afternoon. Dr. THOMAS AMORY was chosen Morning Preacher there in his stead; and upon Dr. Amory's death in 1774, JOSEPH TOWERS, LL. D. was invited to the same office, which he still retains.

Dr. ISAAC MADDOX, afterwards Bishop of Worcester, when he had finished his academical studies among the Dissenters, preached occasionally, a few times, at Newington Green, to oblige his aunt, who resided there; but he never accepted of any Dissenting congregation.

APPENDIX, N° IV. (see p. 35.)

About the month of June 1709, great numbers of poor Palatines, Swabians, and other Germans, most of them Protestants, being driven from their habitations, either by the oppressive exactions of the French, or the desolation of their country, occasioned by the calamities of war, began to come over into this kingdom, insomuch that by the middle of the month they were increased to 6520. Totally destitute and unprovided as they were, they must have perished, had not the Queen ordered a daily allowance to be distributed to them, and a sufficient number of tents to be delivered out of the Tower for their encamping on Blackheath and a large field near Camberwell. There was afterwards a brief granted for collecting money for their subsistence throughout the whole kingdom. Those that were Roman Catholicks

tholicks were sent back again; of such as remained, some were entertained in private families, others disposed of to several parishes which were allowed for them 5*l.* a head, many were sent to Ireland, where the parliament voted 24000*l*. for their reception, a few to Carolina, but the greater number, 2700, were shipped to New York, where they arrived with colonel Robert Hunter *, the governor, June 14, 1710. They were allowed 10 acres of land only to one family, and meeting with unkind treatment there, generally removed to Pennsylvania, where they had better encouragement, and where many of their descendants still remain. It is painful to comment on the illiberal spirit of our ancestors; but truth obliges me to observe, that this unhappy people, in many instances, met with treatment highly disgraceful to the English nation, and to humanity itself. A clamour was excited against them, and corn being at that time 10*s.* a bushel, the multitude were taught to hate and despise them.

"Those who advised the bringing in the Palatines," says Swift in one of his Examiners, "were enemies to the kingdom;" and in another of those papers he adds, "Some persons, whom the voice of the nation authorized me to call her ene-
"mies, taking advantage of the general naturalization act, had invited over a great
"number of foreigners of all religions, under the name of Palatines, who under-
"stood no trade or handicraft, yet rather chose to beg than labour; who, besides
"infesting our streets, bred contagious diseases, by which we lost in natives thrice
"the number of what we gained in foreigners. The House of Commons, as a re-
"medy against this evil, brought in a bill for repealing that act of general natura-
"lization; which, to the surprize of most people, was rejected by the lords. And
"upon this occasion I must allow myself to have been justly rebuked by one of my
"weekly monitors, for pretending, in a former paper, to hope that law would be
"repealed; wherein the Commons being disappointed, took care however to send
"many of the Palatines away, and to represent their being invited over as perni-
"cious counsel." To the same purpose, in his "History of the Four last Years of
"Queen Anne," the Dean repeats, "Whether bringing over the Palatines were a
"mere consequence of this law for a general naturalization, or whether, as many
"surmized, it had some other meaning; it appeared manifestly, by the issue, that
"the publick was a loser by every individual among them; and that a kingdom can
"no more be the richer by such an importation, than a man can be fatter by a wen,
"which is unsightly and troublesome at best, and intercepts that nourishment which
"would otherwise diffuse itself through the whole body."

Justice requires me to add, that, by an act passed in the parliament of Great Britain, 1 George I. c. 29, they were not thought an idle or useless people in the kingdom of Ireland. Those who settled in Pennsylvania invited numbers of their countrymen to join them, and scarce a year passed but many thousands went over. By these means the province of Pennsylvania became enriched to such a degree, that land which might have been purchased for 100*l*. soon rose to treble the value, and the people of that district were amply rewarded for their kindness and liberality. Among other schemes for employing them, one was to divide New Forest into lots and shares.

* Of whom a particular account is given in the "History of Croyland," p. 78

APPENDIX, N° V.

ADDITIONS and CORRECTIONS.

P. 8, l. 13, r. Edward Stillingfleet, D. D. of St. John's College, Cambridge; rector of Sutton, Bedfordshire, 1657 *, which he resigned for the rectory of St. Andrew, Holborn, Jan. 1664-5; preacher at the Rolls Chapel; prebendary of Islington, Feb. 9, 1666-7; canon residentiary of St. Paul's, 1670; exchanged his prebend for this of Newington, Oct. 11, 1672, archdeacon of London, 1676; dean of St. Paul's, 1677, consecrated bishop of Worcester, Oct. 13, 1689, died March 27, 1699.

P. 17. The Author desires to suggest a doubt, whether he is not mistaken in asserting that Dr. Simpson was a writer in Ecclesiastical Controversy, as he is uncertain whether the person referred to was not a Clergyman of the same name, who died in 1658, and might possibly be the Doctor's father.

Ib. l. 20, Mr. Hunt died in August 1703.

Ib. l. 26, r. and vicar of Northall in Middlesex.

P. 21, note, l. 5, 6, r. his eldest son *was* John Sutton.

P. 22. Robert Dudley earl of Leicester bore, 1. Or, a Lion rampant queue fourchée, Vert, for *Dudley*. 2. Or, two Lions passant in pale, Azure, *Somery*. 3. Gules, a cinquefoil Ermine, for *Bellomont* earl of Leicester. 4. Argent, a cross patonce, Azure, for *Malpas*. 5. Barry of six, Argent and Azure, in chief three Torteauxes, for *Edward Grey* viscount Lisle. 6. Or, a maunch, Gules, for *Hastings* earl of Huntingdon. 7. Barry of ten, Argent and Azure, six martlets in orle, Gules, *Valence* earl of Pembroke. 8. Vair, Or and Gules, for *Ferrers* earl of Derby. 9. Gules, seven mascles conjoined, Or, *Ferrers* of Groby, and *Quincy* earl of Winton. 10. Sable, three garbes Argent, for *Dermot Mac Murrough* king of Leinster. 11. Gules, a Lion rampant and border ingrailed, Or, *Talbot* earl of Shrewsbury. 12. Gules, a fess between six cross croslets, Or, *Beauchamp* earl of Warwick. 13. Chequée, Or and Azure, a chevron Ermine, for *Thomas de Newburgh* earl of Warwick. 14. Gules, a chevron between ten crosses patée, Argent, for *Berkley*. 15. Gules, a Lion passant guardant, Argent, crowned Or, for *Warine Fitz-Gerald*. 16. Or, a fess between two chevrons Sable, for the lords *Lisle*.

P. 40, l. 10, dele the article about Dr. Wright's son, for he had only one daughter.

* He was succeeded at Sutton by the Rev. William Stephens, who enjoyed that rectory 56 years, and died in 1721, as appears by the inscription upon his grave-stone in the chancel, and was succeeded by the Rev. Matthias Haynes. This Mr. William Stephens was the publisher of "A Letter to the Author of the Memorial of the State of England," written by Thomas Rawlins, esq. 1705, and refusing to be an evidence against Mr. Rawlins, he was sentenced to stand in the pillory, but the sentence was afterwards remitted. Biog. Brit. vol. VI. under Toland, p. 3972.

FINIS.

ERRATA.

P. 5, l. 5, For 1300, read Feb. 1303-4.
    8, For 1307, read Nov. 28, 1308.
  7, l. 17, Read Can*ter*bury.
  8, l. 18, Before Dec. infert " collated to this prebend."
12, The date of Dr. Wright's death is 3 non. April.
17, l. 7, Read 1656 or 7.
    23, Add this note: The collection of Roman, Britifh, Runic, Saxon, and Englifh coins and medals, the manufcripts, curiofities, &c. of the learned Mr. Ralph Thorefby, which after his death came into the poffeffion of his fon, were fold by auction, by Whifton Briftow, on the 5th, 6th, and 7th of March, 1764.
18, l. 9, For B. D. read M. A.
26, The note fhould be referred to James Abney, efq. p. 25, l. ult. *whofe* eldeft fon Sir Edward is thought to have been, and therefore brother to Sir Thomas, lord of this manor *jure uxoris*.
50, N° 4 of the Appendix fhould be referred to p. 33.
52, l. 14, For Ib. l. 20, read P. 8, l. 20.
    22, For Huntington, read Pembroke.

LaVergne, TN USA
24 February 2011

217755LV00003B/117/P